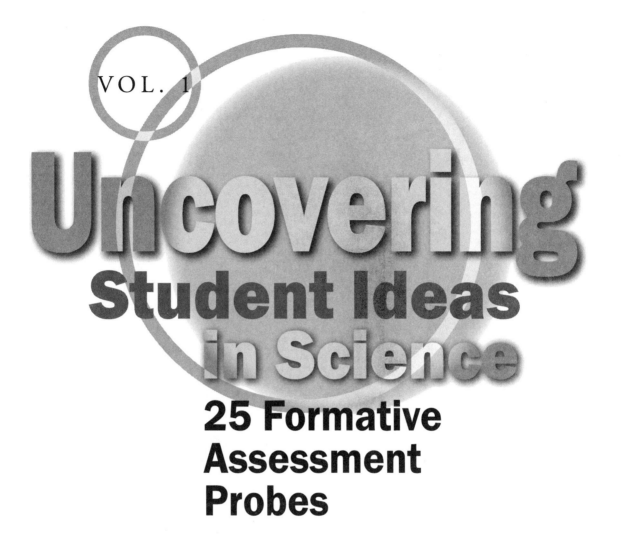

VOL. 1

# Uncovering
## Student Ideas
## in Science

**25 Formative Assessment Probes**

VOL. 1

# Uncovering
## Student Ideas
## in Science

# 25 Formative Assessment Probes

By Page Keeley,
Francis Eberle,
and Lynn Farrin

NSTApress
NATIONAL SCIENCE TEACHERS ASSOCIATION
Arlington, Virginia

NATIONAL SCIENCE TEACHERS ASSOCIATION

Claire Reinburg, Director
Judy Cusick, Senior Editor
Andrew Cocke, Associate Editor
Betty Smith, Associate Editor
Robin Allan, Book Acquisitions Coordinator

Cover, Inside Design, and Illustrations by Linda Olliver

PRINTING AND PRODUCTION Catherine Lorrain-Hale, Director
    Nguyet Tran, Assistant Production Manager
    Jack Parker, Electronic Prepress Technician

NATIONAL SCIENCE TEACHERS ASSOCIATION
Gerald F. Wheeler, Executive Director
David Beacom, Publisher

LIBRARY OF CONGRESS CATALOGING-IN-PUBLICATION DATA

Keeley, Page.
Uncovering student ideas in science / by Page Keeley, Francis Eberle, and Lynn Farrin.
    v. cm.
Includes bibliographical references and index.
Contents: v. 1. 25 formative assessment probes
ISBN 0-87355-255-5
1.  Science--Study and teaching. 2.  Educational evaluation.  I. Eberle, Francis. II. Farrin, Lynn.
III. Title.
Q181.K248 2005
507'.1--dc22
                        2005018770

*NSTA is committed to publishing material that promotes the best in inquiry-based science education.
However, conditions of actual use may vary, and the safety procedures and practices described in this book are
intended to serve only as a guide. Additional precautionary measures may be required. NSTA and the authors
do not warrant or represent that the procedures and practices in this book meet any safety code or standard
of federal, state, or local regulations. NSTA and the authors disclaim any liability for personal injury or
damage to property arising out of or relating to the use of this book, including any of the recommendations,
instructions, or materials contained therein.*

Permission is granted in advance for photocopying brief excerpts for one-time use in a classroom or
workshop. Requests involving electronic reproduction should be directed to Permissions/NSTA Press,
1840 Wilson Blvd., Arlington, VA 22201-3000; fax 703-526-9754. Permissions requests for coursepacks,
textbooks, and other commercial uses should be directed to Copyright Clearance Center, 222 Rosewood
Dr., Danvers, MA 01923; fax 978-646-8600; *www.copyright.com*.

*Featuring sciLINKS®—a new way of connecting text and the internet. Up-to-the-minute online
content, classroom ideas, and other materials are just a click away.*

# Contents

## Preface

## Introduction

## Physical Science Assessment Probes

# Life, Earth, and Space Science
# Assessment Probes

# Preface

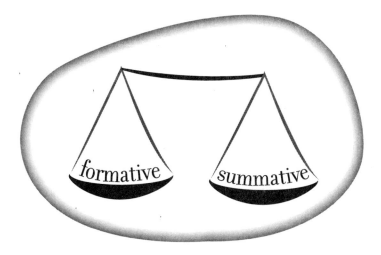

## Overview

Assessment is one of the most pervasive and complex issues dominating today's education landscape. Assessments that document and measure the extent of student achievement are summative in nature. Formative assessments are used to gather information about student learning throughout the teaching and learning process. This information is used to adjust instruction as well as to provide feedback to students. Too often the term *assessment* is used synonymously with the end products of instruction and student learning such as quizzes, tests, performance tasks, and standardized tests. This misconception about the use and types of assessment minimizes its complex nature, stages, and purposes (Atkin and Coffey 2003, p. xi).

In the recent urgency to meet federal, state, and district mandates for greater accountability, the amount of time, resources, and emphasis on assessment has tilted considerably toward the summative side. This "weighted" shift toward summative assessment has led to more standardized testing of students, often with only marginal gains in achievement. When student test scores fail to rise significantly, the usual response has been to repeat the cycle of more testing and test preparation. This cycle reduces the time teachers spend on identifying problematic areas of student learning at the beginning of instruction and monitoring for conceptual change.

On the other side of the assessment scale, formative assessment, when used deliberately and effectively, helps teachers find out what

# Preface

their students think and know at the beginning and throughout an instructional sequence. One way teachers use this assessment information is to adjust and monitor learning and to determine when students are ready to demonstrate their learning. This type of formative assessment, which is the form of assessment addressed in this book, is inextricably linked to instruction.

Recent studies and reports validate the need to place more emphasis on formative assessment in order to create a balanced system of assessment in science classrooms (Black and Harrison 2004; Black and Wiliam 1998; Bransford, Brown, and Cocking 1999). The need to balance the assessment scale by transferring some of the weight to the formative assessment side is as urgent and may be more effective in improving achievement in the long run than the short-term demand to raise test scores. Results from national and international studies provide compelling evidence that the purposeful use of formative assessment improves student learning in science, particularly with low-performing groups. These results include evidence that when formative assessment is used well, it can actually help to raise students' test scores (Black et al. 2003).

In addition, a recent report on educational assessment from the National Research Council included the recommendation that "the balance of mandates and resources should be shifted from an emphasis on external forms of assessment to an increased emphasis on classroom formative assessment designed to assist learning" (Pelligrino, Chudowsky, and Glaser 2001, p. 14).

This book reflects efforts by the authors to provide support and resources to teachers for just one of the purposes of formative assessment. The formative assessment emphasized in this book is for learning about students' ideas in order to inform teaching. This type of assessment *for* learning is grounded in research and is based on one of the foundational ideas in *How People Learn: Brain, Mind, Experience, and School*: "Students come to the classroom with preconceptions about how the world works. If their initial understanding is not engaged, they may fail to grasp the new concepts and information that are taught, or they may learn for purposes of a test, but revert to their preconceptions outside the classroom" (Bransford, Brown, and Cocking 1999, p. 14).

Assessment, whether it is formative or summative, is not value free as there is no perfect educational practice and hence no perfect educational assessment (Hein and Price 1994). The best we may be able to accomplish, which is an underlying premise of this book, is to achieve balance in assessment. Our hope is that the use and examples of one strategy for formative assessment—the formative assessment probes in this book—contribute to bringing balance into assessment by helping teachers discover the power of knowing what their own students think about core ideas in science and using the information to improve conceptual learning through effective teaching. As Malcolm Gladwell (2000) describes in his book *The Tipping Point: How Little Things Can Make a Big Difference*, the "tipping point" is that magical moment when an idea crosses a threshold, "tips," and spreads like wildfire. It is our hope that the use of these probes will spread among educators, bring a new vitality to assessment and instruction, and tip the scale back in order to balance *assessment for learning* with *assessment of learning*.

## Need for Formative Assessment Tools in Science

Formative assessment has been used routinely over the years by science teachers to find out what their students know and can do. Teachers continue to seek out effective, ready-made, well-designed questions and strategies that will help them to uncover what their students are actually thinking and to build a bridge between those ideas and the scientific ideas articulated in national and state science standards. Once teachers realize the untapped potential of teacher- and student-friendly formative assessment to significantly improve teaching practice, student learning, and even standardized test results, it may eventually become the most pervasive form of assessment in the classroom.

Developing any type of quality assessment or lesson is a challenging and time-intensive process for teachers, who already have full teaching schedules and other responsibilities. To design probing questions that reveal students' preconceptions, teachers need to have good subject matter knowledge, but not necessarily the kind of content knowledge that is developed through an advanced study of science (Black et al. 2003). Effective teachers need to thoroughly understand the basic ideas appropriate for their students, the students' pre-

conceptions, and ways to respond to student thinking. Teachers also need to develop their pedagogical content knowledge (Shulman 1986), knowing the aspects of subject matter that cause students particular difficulties and knowing how to design learning paths to overcome these difficulties.

A wide range of summative assessments and instructional materials is available to science teachers, but few resources provide ready-made science formative assessments that can also enhance and support teachers' pedagogical content knowledge. We call the type of formative assessments provided in this book *probes* and we describe them in more detail in the Introduction. Teachers urgently need this type of field-tested, content-aligned, easy-to-administer, and quick-to-analyze formative assessment.

These probes can be used with different state standards and instructional materials because they are based on core science concepts, most of which cut across multiple grade levels. This book provides 25 assessment probes with supporting background material for teachers that connects the purpose for which the assessment was designed with key concepts, content explanations, developmental considerations, national standards, research on learning, suggested instructional strategies, and additional resources so that they may be used by any teacher in any instructional context.

## Development and Use of the Probes

The assessment probes included in this book were purposely developed to elicit students'

# Preface

thinking about specific ideas in science. Several of these ideas have been identified as difficult for students to learn due to their abstract or counterintuitive nature. The probes were not designed to be used for summative purposes, but rather as a sort of "temperature taking" to inform instruction. Each probe has been field tested with several teachers and classes of diverse student backgrounds and revised in order to effectively target the specific idea(s) the probe is designed to uncover. The field tests included hundreds of students across multiple grade levels, allowing the field testers to identify grade levels at which students' ideas are beginning to develop as well as grade levels at which certain ideas, though taught previously, have not been learned.

We do not claim that the assessment probes in this book are reliable and valid assessment items in the technical sense that is needed for summative assessment purposes. They are designed to find out what students think about particular foundational concepts identified in the national standards and cognitive research literature. (Note: By "national standards," we are referring here and throughout the book to *National Science Education Standards* [NRC 1996] and to *Benchmarks for Science Literacy* [AAAS 1993].) In many cases, there is no one "right" answer. It is the students' explanations that reveal the students' thinking about the ideas and provide insight to the teachers as to next steps for instruction. The specific ideas targeted by a probe may or may not be included in a particular teacher's or grade level's curriculum; however, they can still be used to gather data that will inform instruction of related ideas, trace the development of thinking across multiple grade levels, or determine whether instruction in prior grade levels helped students develop scientific ideas. Although some of the probes target a specific grade-level standard, we would caution against using these probes as a summative assessment of students. Rather, the assessment probes included in this volume can provide information about

- How students' ideas may differ from one grade level to the next
- How ready individual students are for instruction
- Ideas students have before instruction
- Whether conceptual change is occurring
- Whether students retain the accepted scientific ideas years after instruction or revert back to their prior knowledge
- Gaps that exist in a school's or district's curriculum

The probes included in this book were not designed for use in a traditional research context with control groups or in comparisons before and after instruction. While our focus is on helping teachers learn more about their students' ideas for the purpose of improving instruction, the probes could be used for practitioner research into student thinking. The probes can serve as a bridge between formal research findings about students' ideas and their practical application in the science classroom.

## Next Steps

This book is planned as a series of assessment probe books, each volume describing a new application as well as including new probes. In the next volume of *Uncovering Student Ideas in Science*, we will describe strategies for using the probes during instruction to help your students experience conceptual change. In the third volume, we will address ways to use the probes for professional development.

## References

American Association for the Advancement of Science (AAAS). 1993. *Benchmarks for science literacy.* New York: Oxford University Press.

Atkin, J. M., and J. E. Coffey, eds. 2003. *Everyday assessment in the science classroom.* Arlington, VA: NSTA Press.

Black, P., and C. Harrison. 2004. *Science inside the black box.* London: nferNelson.

Black, P., and D. Wiliam. 1998. Inside the black box: Raising standards through classroom assessment. *Phi Delta Kappan* 80 (2): 139–148.

Black, P., C. Harrison, C. Lee, B. Marshall, and D. Wiliam. 2003. *Assessment for learning: Putting it into practice.* Berkshire, England: Open University Press.

Bransford, J. D., A. L. Brown, and R. R. Cocking, eds. 1999. *How people learn: Brain, mind, experience, and school.* Washington, DC: National Academy Press.

Gladwell, M. 2000. *The tipping point: How little things can make a big difference.* Boston, MA: Little, Brown.

Hein, G., and S. Price. 1994. *Active assessment for active science.* Portsmouth, NH: Heinemann.

National Research Council (NRC). 1996. *National science education standards.* Washington, DC: National Academy Press.

Pelligrino, J., N. Chudowsky, and R. Glaser. 2001. *Knowing what students know: The science and design of educational assessment.* Washington, DC: National Academy Press.

Shulman, L. 1986. Those who understand: Knowledge growth in teaching. *Educational Researcher* 15 (1): 4–14.

## Acknowledgments

The assessment probes in this book have been extensively field tested and piloted with hundreds of students in Maine, New Hampshire, and Vermont by the Maine Mathematics and Science Alliance (MMSA). We would like to thank the teachers in the National Science Foundation–funded Northern New England Co-Mentoring Network (NNECN) (*www.nnecn.org*), Maine's Governor's Academy for Science Education Leadership, and participants in various MMSA professional development programs for their willingness to field test and pilot items, share student data, and contribute ideas for additional assessment probe development. In particular we would like to acknowledge the following teachers for their contributions to this project:

Judith Allard, VT; Dr. Pasco Avery, ME; Julie Barry, ME; Mary Belisle, ME; Anita Bernhardt, ME; Lise Boefinger, NH; Tracy Bricchi, NH; Ruth Bither-Broene, ME; Linda Brasseur, VT; Nancy Chesley, ME; Gay

# Preface

Craig, VT; Lisa Damian-Marvin, ME; Linda D'apolito, ME; Laurette Darling, ME; Steve Deangelis, ME; Mary Dunn, ME; Dalene Dutton, ME; Sandra Ferland, ME; Barbara Fortier, ME; Sharon Gallant, ME; Lauree Gott, ME; Anne Guerriero, NH; Douglas Hodhum, NH; Erin Hubbard, NH; Anita Hopkins, ME; Ricia Hyde, ME; Lisa Jerals, ME; Vincent Johnson, ME; Kathleen King, ME; Peggy Labrosse, NH; Axel Larson, ME; Cindy Langdon, ME; Gary LaShure, VT; Christine Mara, ME; Wes Marble, ME; Margo Murphy, ME; Andrew Njaa, ME; Laurie Olmsted, ME; Dr. Lois Ongley, ME; Jack O'Reilly, NH; Beth Paradis, ME; Tia Pass, ME; LuAnn Pigeon, NH; Ingrid Porter, ME; Andrew Sarto, ME; Greg Renner, VT; Steven Rice, ME; Suzi Seluki, ME; Katy Snider, NH; Emily Stuart, ME; Ingrid Thomas, ME; Jane Voth-Palisi, NH; J. David White, ME; Mary Whitten, ME.

We also thank the following individuals for their reviews of this book: Richard Audet, associate professor of science education, Roger Williams University; Mistilina Sato, assistant professor of teacher development and science education, University of Minnesota, Twin Cities; and Joyce Tugel, science specialist, Eisenhower Regional Alliance at TERC, Cambridge, MA.

## About the Authors

Page Keeley, senior science program director, Francis Eberle, executive director, and Lynn Farrin, science associate, all work at the Maine Mathematics and Science Alliance (MMSA) in Augusta, Maine, where they develop, support, and coordinate various science education initiatives throughout Maine and northern New England. Combined, they have a total of over 25 years of teaching experience in middle and high school science; Page and Francis have also served as adjunct instructors in the University of Maine system. Their work with teachers, schools, and organizations includes the areas of professional development, leadership, standards, curriculum development, assessment, and school reform. The authors currently serve as PIs, co-PIs, and senior personnel on four National Science Foundation grants, actively serve on state and national advisory boards and committees, and frequently present their work at National Science Teachers Association conventions.

# Introduction

> The most important single factor influencing learning is what the learner knows. Ascertain this and teach accordingly.
> —David Ausubel, *Educational Psychology: A Cognitive View*

## Classroom Assessment

*In the broadest sense of the word, assessment is something we do all the time. We encounter a new situation, make a judgment about what is happening, and decide what to do next. The evidence of our encounters continually shapes and reshapes our actions. Our actions may be more effective if we are flexible—that is, if we are prepared to modify our intentions in light of events. They might also be more effective if we probe the situation carefully in order to ensure that we understand what is going on before jumping to conclusions.* (Black et al. 2003, p. 6)

Classroom assessment occurs every day, most often as formative assessment. "The first thing that comes to mind for many people when they think of 'classroom assessment' is a midterm or end of course exam, used by the teacher for summative grading purposes. But such practices represent only a fraction of the kinds of assessments that occur on an ongoing basis in an effective classroom" (Pelligrino, Chudowsky, and Glaser 2001, p. 225). Everyday classroom assessment is unique to your classroom context. It depends more on the skills, knowledge, and priorities you and your students have than on any particular protocol or strategy (Atkin and Coffey 2003, p. xi). Throughout the course of a unit or lesson, you assess students using various formats, including individual, small-group, or whole-class elicitation questions; student interviews; observations; informal conversations; journaling; performance tasks; even traditional assessments such as quizzes or tests during or after a lesson.

Classroom assessment is continuous and

# Introduction

provides you with a rich set of data about student learning. However, for the assessment to be considered "formative," you must use the data to modify your curriculum, alter your teaching, or provide feedback to your students. Classroom assessment serves multiple purposes, including diagnosing, monitoring, providing feedback, and measuring. Each of these assessment purposes links to various stages in your instructional sequence as described in Figure 1.

A key stage in the instructional sequence is *elicitation*. Elicitation gives students the opportunity to make their ideas and reasons explicit as they begin the study of a unit topic. It engages them and also alerts them to what they will be thinking and learning about in the upcoming instruction. "By providing the opportunity to articulate their initial conceptions and to clarify these ideas, the elicitation questions and subsequent discussions help stu-

dents begin building new, more powerful conceptions" (Minstrell and van Zee 2003, p. 62). In a similar vein, another group of researchers put it this way:

> *Knowledge of children's learning and the development of expertise clearly indicates that assessment practices should focus on making students' thinking visible to themselves and to others by drawing out their current understandings so that instructional strategies can be selected to support an appropriate course for future learning. In particular, assessment practices should focus on identifying the preconceptions children bring to learning settings.* (Pelligrino, Chudowsky, and Glaser 2001, p. 91)

Using the probes provided in this book at the elicitation and exploration and concept development stages of instruction is consistent with the current research on how students learn and with recommendations for

## Figure 1   Purposes and Stages of Classroom Assessment

| Type of Classroom Assessment | Purpose | Link to Stage in an Instructional Sequence |
|---|---|---|
| Formative (pre-instruction) | Diagnostic—to find out students' existing ideas | Elicitation Stage—Used prior to developing instruction or during the instructional sequence when new ideas are encountered. |
| Formative | To monitor student learning and/or to provide feedback to students on their learning | Exploration and Concept Development Stage—Used continuously throughout the instructional sequence. |
| Summative | To measure the extent to which students have achieved a learning goal | Application Stage—Used primarily at the end of an instructional sequence. |
| Note: The assessment probes provided in this book are formative in nature and are designed to be used during the elicitation and exploration and concept development stages of an instructional sequence. | | |

using assessment for learning and informing instruction.

## What Is a Formative Assessment Probe?

The assessment examples in this book, which we call *probes*, are formative in nature. They are used primarily for diagnostic and monitoring purposes. They are assessments *for* learning, not assessments *of* learning. While several of these probes could indeed serve to summatively assess your students' learning, their primary purpose is not to measure the extent to which your students achieved proficiency in science subject matter knowledge, but rather to reveal the types of conceptions your students have about common science concepts before and throughout instruction. "Students enter the study of science with a vast array of such preconceptions based on their everyday experiences. Teachers will need to engage those ideas if students are to understand science" (Donovan and Bransford 2005, p. 399). The probes in this book shift the focus from measuring and documenting student learning to examining student thinking for the purpose of informing teaching and learning.

This book focuses on formative assessments that will enable you to probe for and quickly and efficiently examine a multitude of possible ideas your students hold, including misconceptions, naive thoughts, and incomplete ideas. (Many educators and researchers prefer to collectively call these ideas *alternative frameworks* rather than *misconceptions*—meaning that students' ideas are not always wrong, even though they may differ from those of a

scientist [Sneider 2003].) The probes also uncover the correct ideas your students hold and the critical-thinking and reasoning strategies they use to support their ideas. These strategies can be based on intuition, logic, everyday experiences, or scientific knowledge.

Why is it important for you to take the time to uncover the preconceptions your students have? Research has shown that preconceived ideas in science develop early in a student's K–12 experience and can be tenacious (Donovan and Bransford 2005; Bransford, Brown, and Cocking 1999). Through their daily, informal experiences with objects and phenomena, students develop ideas and schema for organizing and explaining scientific concepts even before they are formally taught scientific ideas in school. Sometimes these ideas are congruent with scientific knowledge. Other times they conflict with the scientific view. This formation of students' own conceptions, which may be correct, partially correct, or incorrect, continues throughout their K–12 school years regardless of whether or not the ideas are taught in science class. If these ideas are ignored, they may get in the way when new ideas are introduced. They simply do not go away, even as students progress from elementary grades to middle school and even into high school and adulthood. Surprisingly, many of the probes in this book reveal that high school students have partially understood ideas and misconceptions that are not much different from those of their elementary school counterparts.

Thus, a major challenge for science teachers is to build conceptual bridges from stu-

# Introduction

dents' own ideas to scientifically accepted views. To do this, you must know what your students' starting points are so that you can provide experiences that support the development of correct conceptual understanding.

The science assessment probes in this book are field-tested formative assessments that are based on core concepts and ideas in science, many of which cut across multiple grade spans at increasing levels of sophistication. The probes are designed to help you identify students' ideas at various stages during their K–12 experiences. For example, elementary students may have basic notions about atoms, molecules, or "tiny bits," but it is not until later in middle school that students are expected to use the idea of atoms and molecules to explain phenomena. Knowing the ideas students have at different grade levels can give you a clear picture of conceptual change over time.

These probes are intended to be used before and during instruction. Finding out students' ideas, examining them carefully, and using the information obtained from the probes are integral aspects of formative assessment. It is this latter aspect of using the assessment data that is most overlooked in classroom assessment. It is not sufficient to know the misconceptions your students may have. Information from the assessment probes will have little impact unless you make changes in curriculum and instruction based on where students are in their thinking.

## Assessment Probe Design and Features

The formative assessment probes included in this book are designed to address several of the student learning difficulties identified in the research literature. In areas where there is little or no research, they have been designed to address problematic areas identified by teachers. Each probe consists of two parts to be completed by the student: a selected response and a justification for selecting the response.

The first part is introduced by an engaging prompt about a familiar phenomenon or objects. The prompt is followed by a question that asks students to select from a set of likely student-held responses. These responses include research-identified ideas, including misconceptions, or common ideas that emerged through the probe field testing. Students' selected responses provide a quick snapshot for you to see what individual students think about an idea. This data can be quickly tallied to get a picture of where your class stands as far as the variety of ideas students have.

The second part of each probe asks students to describe their thinking or provide an explanation or "rule" they used to select their answer. *Rule* is a general term used with younger students (though not limited to younger students) that usually involves a set of basic criteria students use to categorize or make sense of an object or phenomena. For example, in deciding whether certain materials are considered matter or not matter, a student might explain how she used the rule that "it had to be something she could feel and see" to sort objects and materials.

Asking students to describe a rule often leads to uncovering intuitive rules, such as "more A, more B" (Stavy and Tirosh 2000). This rule simply means if you have more of something (such as mass or volume), then other characteristics increase (such as density and boiling point). This rule may be applied in a variety of physical, Earth, and biological contexts and seems to be a core conception that contributes to several common misconceptions. Older students may provide more sophisticated scientific explanations that link a claim with evidence and reasoning strategies to support their answers. In both types of justification, involving either rules or explanations, students provide a rationale for their ideas, giving teachers a detailed glimpse into their thinking.

To develop the probes we used a process and formats described in *Science Curriculum Topic Study: Bridging the Gap Between Standards and Practice* (Keeley 2005). The process begins with identifying the concepts and related ideas in a topic, based on a study of the national standards and research. The concepts and ideas in the standards are then linked to the concepts and ideas addressed in the cognitive research literature and to their associated learning difficulties and misconceptions.

The national standards used to identify the concepts and specific ideas were from *Benchmarks for Science Literacy* (AAAS 1993) and *National Science Education Standards* (NRC 1996). The sources of research summaries were *Benchmarks for Science Literacy* (Chapter 15, "The Research Base") and *Making Sense of Secondary Science: Research into Children's Ideas* (Driver et al. 1994). (Note: The latter resource does not address only high school science. *Secondary science* is a term used in the United Kingdom to describe grade levels beyond early primary grades. The book addresses ideas from grade 1 through adulthood and includes preK–2 ideas in several examples.) Figure 2 shows an example of how the process was used to "unpack" the topic "conservation of matter" in order to match the concepts and ideas in that topic to the research findings. This information was then used to develop a set of assessment probes that target standards and research-based ideas related to conservation of matter.

In Figure 2, the shaded areas designate the specific Benchmarks idea and the related research finding that were used to develop the probe "Ice Cubes in a Bag" (p. 49). Even though the idea in the national standards is a K–2 idea, the probe can be used with higher grade levels to determine if students use the more sophisticated ideas of closed systems or numbers of atoms. Other matches between the research ideas and the standards led to the development of three additional probes in the conservation of matter set ("Lemonade," "Cookie Crumbles," and "Seedlings in a Jar").

The probes are designed to provide you with quick and targeted feedback on students' ideas and learning. The data from the first part of the probe are easy to collect and organize. Individuals or teams of teachers can quantify the data by making charts or graphs that show student results that can be shared with colleagues across grade levels. As you read the students' explanations, you will notice similar

# Introduction

**Figure 2  Mapping Grades 3–8 Conservation of Matter Related Concepts and Ideas to Research Findings for Probe Development[a]**

| Science Concepts and Ideas | Research Findings |
|---|---|
| **Properties**<br>• Objects have many observable properties, including size, weight, and shape. Those properties can be measured using tools such as rulers and balances. (NSES K–4, p. 127)<br>• Materials can exist in different states—solid, liquid, and gas. (NSES K–4, p. 127)<br>• Air is a substance that surrounds us, takes up space, and whose movements we feel as wind. (BSL 3–5, p. 68)<br><br>**Physical and Chemical Change**<br>• Water can be a liquid or solid and can go back and forth from one form to another. If water is turned into ice and then ice is allowed to melt, the amount of water is the same as it was before freezing. (BSL K–2, p. 67)<br>• No matter how parts of an object are assembled, the weight of the whole object made is always the same as the sum of the parts; and when a thing is broken into parts, the parts have the same total weight as the original thing. (BSL 3–5, p. 77)<br>• Substances react chemically in characteristic ways with other substances to form new substances with different characteristic properties. In chemical reactions, the total mass is conserved. (NSES 5–8, p. 154)<br><br>**Intractions in a Closed System**<br>• No matter how substances within a closed system interact with one another, or how they combine or break apart, the total mass of the system remains the same. (BSL 6–8, p. 79)<br><br>**Particulate Matter**<br>• The idea of atoms explains the conservation of matter: If the number of atoms stays the same no matter how they are rearranged, then their total mass stays the same. (BSL 6–8, p. 79) | **Matter and Its Properties**<br>• Students need to have a concept of matter in order to understand conservation of matter. (BSL, p. 336)<br>• Students need to accept weight as an intrinsic property of matter to use weight conservation reasoning. (BSL, p. 336)<br>• Confusion between weight and density contributes to difficulty understanding conservation of matter. (BSL, p. 336)<br>• The concept of mass develops slowly. Mass is often associated with the phonetically similar word *massive* and thus may be equated with an increase in size or volume. (Driver et al., p. 78)<br>• The idea that gases possess material character is difficult. Students may not regard gases as having weight or mass. Until they accept gas as a substance, they are unlikely to conserve mass in changes that involve gases. (Driver et al., p. 80)<br><br>**Physical and Chemical Change**<br>• There is often a discrepancy between weight and matter conservation with dissolving. Some students accept the idea that the substance is still there but the weight is negligible, is "up in the water," or it no longer weighs anything. (Driver et al., p. 84)<br>• Some students believe one state of matter of the same substance has more or less weight than a different state. (Driver et al., p. 80)<br>• In changes that involve a gas, students are more apt to understand matter is conserved if the gas is visible (BSL, p. 337)<br>• Weight conservation during chemical reactions is more difficult for students to understand, particularly if a gas is involved. (BSL, p. 337)<br>• Many students do not view chemical changes as interactions. They have difficulty understanding the idea that substances can form from a recombination of the original atoms. (BSL, p. 337)<br>• Students have more difficulty with the quantitative aspect of chemical change and conservation. (Driver et al., p. 88)<br>• The way a student perceives a chemical or physical change may determine whether he or she understands matter is conserved. For example, if it looks as if something has disappeared or spread out more, then students may think the mass changes. (Driver et al., p. 77)<br><br>**Particle Ideas**<br>• Newly constructed ideas of atoms may undermine conservation reasoning. For example, if a material is seen as being dispersed in very small particles, then it may be regarded as having negligible weight or being more spread out and less heavy. (Driver et al., p. 77) |

*Note:* NSES = National Research Council. 1996. *National science education standards.* Washington, DC: National Academy Press. BSL = American Association for the Advancement of Science. 1993. *Benchmarks for science literacy.* New York: Oxford University Press. Driver et al. = Driver, R., A. Squires, P. Rushworth, and V. Wood-Robinson. 1994. *Making sense of secondary science: Research into children's ideas.* London and New York: RoutledgeFalmer.

[a] The shaded items are the specific Benchmark idea and the related research finding that were used to develop the probe "Ice Cubes in a Bag."

ideas held by a number of students as well as idiosyncratic ones held by individual students. Overall, the quick and easy snapshot you can glean from the probe results can inform adjustments to curriculum and instruction in order to improve student learning. Sometimes these adjustments can be made in your classroom. Other times the results can provide valuable information to teachers who have had some of the same students before you or will have them after you.

## Formative Assessment Probes in This Book

The probes in this book are "enhanced selected-response" items. In other words, students must choose from a predetermined list of responses that may match their thinking and then justify their reasons for choosing that response. The probes begin with the selected-choice option. The distracters are particularly useful in determining if your own students' "misconceptions" match those found in the research. The two types of selected-response items are (1) multiple-choice questions with one *best* answer (Note: We don't use the term *correct answer* as it often depends on students' interpretation and reasoning), such as in the probe "Ice Cubes in a Bag" (p. 49), and (2) justified lists, such as used in "Is It Matter?" (p. 79). The multiple-choice questions include a stem that provides students with a familiar phenomenon or object to explain an idea, contrasts opposing views, or provides a situation where students commit to a prediction. Justified lists begin with a statement about objects,

materials, or phenomena, followed by multiple examples students select from that match their ideas related to the statement. Justified lists are particularly helpful in determining if students can transfer their learning from one context to another and what rules or explanations they use to base their selected choices on. For example, in "Making Sound" (p. 43), if students learned about sound and vibration in the context of making musical instruments, they may select mostly items on the list that are similar to musical instruments rather than generalizing their knowledge across contexts.

The probes are also designed not to cue students too much, so that you can gain the most information from their original thinking. For example, in "Making Sound," the task refers to objects that make sound but does not mention the air or other material contacting or surrounding the objects that also vibrates. Evidence of recognizing and using this knowledge in their explanation or rule may not be evident if the students were cued to this idea. A major challenge in developing these probes was to provide just enough detail and appropriate language without putting ideas into students' heads or perpetuating their misconceptions.

The probes in this book are paper-and-pencil tasks. However, they also lend themselves to oral questioning prompts for small- or large-group discussion, card sorts, and individual interviews. Alternative ways to administer the probes to students are explained in the teacher notes accompanying each probe. Probes can easily be adapted to include language and examples that may be more appropriate at a given

# Introduction

grade level. You are encouraged to modify the probes to best fit your students.

## Using the Probes

"Students bring conceptions of everyday phenomena to the classroom that are quite sensible, but scientifically limited or incorrect" (Donovan and Bransford 2005, p. 399). Many of these preconceptions are based on students' everyday experiences outside the classroom, things they hear or see in the media, and ideas that go unchallenged in school settings. Teachers need to engage students in sharing these ideas if students are to understand science. One way to begin this engagement is to provide a probe and ask students to write down their ideas in response to the prompt. Writing a response to the prompt is one method of making students' thinking visible and engaging them in the ideas they will be learning about. At the same time it encourages your students to pay careful attention to the reasoning they use to support their ideas.

The probes can also be used orally to engage small or large groups of students in discussion. Using a probe to elicit individual ideas and then asking students to share and discuss their ideas with others provides you with valuable assessment information and at the same time enhances student learning. The process of making students' thinking explicit through discourse serves a dual purpose. First, it allows teachers to see what types of ideas students have so they can provide interventions that address misconceptions or provide for further learning opportunities. Second, encouraging students to make their ideas explicit

to others actually promotes learning for both the thinker and those with whom he or she shares the ideas (Black et al. 2003).

Questioning is a key component of science teaching and formative assessment. "In many science classrooms, questioning typically involves a three-turn exchange in which the teacher asks a question, a student answers, and the teacher evaluates the answer" (Minstrell and van Zee 2003, p. 61). In too many other science classrooms, teachers try to get students to accept "the right answer" rather than engaging them in a conversation that elicits their ideas and uses those ideas as the starting point for activities, investigations, demonstrations, and readings. You can avoid the "right answer" approach by using the probes to uncover your students' conceptions at any time during an instructional sequence and holding back on giving students an answer so they can discover it for themselves.

Probes also "turn the spotlight from examining students' work to examining teachers' work" (Sneider 2003, p. 39). In other words, they help you understand student thinking so that you can develop more effective ways of teaching. While it is clearly important for you to understand the concepts and skills you teach, "without a way of stepping inside our students' shoes it is impossible for us to communicate those concepts and skills in a deep and meaningful way" (Sneider 2003, p. 39).

The use of assessment probes and their results as a means for determining how to alter curriculum and instruction can be stimulating both personally and professionally. Jim Minstrell, a teacher and researcher well known for his development and use of diagnostic assessment, sums up these rewards in the following quote:

> *When in the classroom I now wear two hats, one as a teacher and another as a researcher studying my students' thinking and how to effect better learning. I can no longer teach without learning about my students' thinking. The more I learn about my students' thinking, the more I can tune my instruction to help students bridge from their initial ideas to more formal, scientific thinking. Rather than merely serving student the activities from the book, we are first using questions to diagnose their thinking. Then, we choose activities to address their thinking. Thinking in this way about our work in the interest of improving our practice is part of what it means to be professional. Teaching never becomes boring— quite the contrary. As teachers, we can expect to be lifelong learners about our profession.*
> (Minstrell and van Zee 2003, p. 72)

The best way to learn how to use a probe is to test one out by giving it to your students and then deciding what to do with the information you have gathered. Try one with your colleagues, too, and together discuss the implications for teaching and learning. Modify the ways you use the probes. In other words, do not always administer the probe as an individual written task. Use the probes during small-group and whole-class discussions and listen carefully to students as they share their ideas. You can use a probe to interview an individual student or have informal conversations with students during nonstructured times.

Feel free to adapt the probes as needed. Some language is problematic for certain students or grade levels. Modify the probe so that it best fits your individual circumstances but, at the same time, do not change it so much that it no longer probes what it was intended for.

Use the teacher notes provided with each probe to consider implications for curriculum and instruction. The format and suggested ideas in the teacher notes provide a framework for summarizing, evaluating, and using the student learning data you collect. Above all, remember that for the probes to be formative you must do something with the data you collect.

## Teacher Notes That Accompany the Probes

Each of the probes in this book contains detailed teacher notes to help you to (a) decide how, when, and with whom to use the assessment probe; (b) link the ideas addressed by the probe to related standards; (c) examine research that informed the development of the probe and that provides additional insight into students' thinking; (d) consider new instructional strategies; and (e) access additional information to learn more about the topic addressed by the probe. We describe the components of the teacher notes below.

### Purpose

"Deciding what to assess is not as simple as it might appear. Existing guidelines for assessment design emphasize that the process should begin with a statement of the purpose for the assessment and a definition of the con-

# Introduction

tent domain to be measured" (Pelligrino, Chudowsky, and Glaser 2001, p. 178). This section describes the concept or general topic for the specific idea the probe is intended to elicit and it describes that idea. It is important that you be clear about what the probe is going to reveal so that you can decide if the probe fits your intended target.

## Related Concepts

A concept is a one-, two-, or three-word mental construct used to organize ideas in a topic (Keeley 2005). Each probe is designed to target one or more related concepts that cut across grade spans. Conversely, multiple probes may address a single concept. You may find it useful to use a cluster of probes to target a concept or specific ideas within a concept. For example, there are four probes that target the concept of conservation of matter. The concept matrices on pages 24 and 116 can help you identify related probes.

## Explanation

A brief scientific explanation accompanies each probe to provide clarification of the scientific content that underlies the probe. The explanations are designed to help you identify what the most scientifically acceptable answers are (sometimes there is not a "right" answer) as well as to clarify any misunderstandings you might have about the content. The explanations are not intended to provide detailed background knowledge on the concept, but enough to connect the idea in the probe with the scientific knowledge it is primarily based

on. If you have a need for further explanation of the content, the teacher notes list National Science Teachers Association (NSTA) resources, such as the *Stop Faking It! Finally Understanding Science So You Can Teach It* series, that will enhance and extend your understanding of the content.

## Curricular and Instructional Considerations

The probes in this book are not limited to one grade level in the way that summative assessments are. Instead, they provide insights into the knowledge and thinking that students in your school may have as they progress from one grade level to the next. Ideas are included that students may not encounter until later in their education (e.g., high school), but teachers in the later grades will come to understand where and how ideas originate. Some of the probes can be used in grades K–12; others may cross over just a few grade levels. Teachers in two different grade spans (e.g., middle and high school) might decide to use the same probe and come together and discuss their findings.

The curricular and instructional considerations also describe how the information gleaned from the probe is useful at a given grade span. For example, the information might be useful for planning instruction when an idea in the probe is a grade-level expectation or it might be useful at a later grade to find out whether students have sufficient prior knowledge to move on to the next level of sophistication. Sometimes the knowledge gained through use of the probe indicates that you might have to back up several grade levels to teach ideas that have not been fully understood in previous grades.

We deliberately chose not to suggest a grade level for each probe. If the probes had been intended to be used for summative purposes, a grade level, aligned with a standard, would have been suggested. However, the probes have a different purpose. Do you want to know about the ideas your students are expected to learn according to your grade-level standards? Are you interested in how preconceived ideas develop and change across multiple grade levels in your school even when they are not yet formally taught? Are you interested in whether students achieved a scientific understanding of previous grade-level ideas before you introduce higher-level concepts? The descriptions of grade-level considerations in this section can be coupled with the section that lists related ideas in the national standards in order to make the best judgment about grade-level use.

## Administering the Probe

Suggestions are provided for administering the probe to students, including a variety of modifications that may make the probe more useful at certain grade spans. For example, the notes might recommend eliminating certain examples from a list for younger students who may not be familiar with particular words or examples, or using the word *weight* instead of *mass* with elementary students. This section may also include suggestions for demonstrating the probe context with artifacts or ways to elicit the probe responses while students interact within a group.

## Related Ideas in *National Science Education Standards* (NRC 1996) and *Benchmarks for Science Literacy* (AAAS 1993)

This section lists the learning goals stated in the two national documents generally considered the "national standards": *National Science Education Standards* (NRC 1996) and *Benchmarks for Science Literacy* (AAAS 1993). Since the probes are not designed as summative assessments, the learning goals listed are not intended to be considered as alignments to the probe, but rather as related ideas. Some targeted ideas, such as a student's conception of matter in "Is It Matter?" (p. 79), are not explicitly stated as learning goals in the standards but are clearly related to national standards concepts such as properties of matter, states of matter, and conservation of matter. When the ideas elicited by a probe appear to be a strong match with a national standard's learning goal, these matches are indicated by a star ★ symbol. You may find this information useful in using probes with lessons and instructional materials that are aligned to national standards and used at a specific grade level.

## Related Research

Each probe is informed by related research where available. Since the probes were not designed primarily for research purposes, an exhaustive literature search was not conducted as part of the development process. The authors

# Introduction

drew on two comprehensive research summaries commonly available to educators: Chapter 15, "The Research Base," in *Benchmarks for Science Literacy* (AAAS 1993) and Rosalind Driver et al.'s *Making Sense of Secondary Science: Research Into Children's Ideas* (1994). Although both of these resources describe studies that have been conducted in past decades, and studied children not only in the United States but in other countries as well, many of the studies' results are considered timeless and universal. (At the same time, however, it is important to recognize that cultural and societal contexts can also influence students' thinking.)

As you use the probes, you are encouraged to seek new and additional research findings. One source of updated research can be found on the Curriculum Topic Study (CTS) website at *www.curriculumtopicstudy.org.* A searchable database on this site links each of the CTS topics to additional research articles and resources.

## Suggestions for Instruction and Assessment

After analyzing your students' responses, it is up to you to decide on the student interventions and instructional planning that would work best in your particular curricular and instructional context. We have included suggestions gathered from the wisdom of teachers, from the knowledge base on effective science teaching, and from our own collective experience as former teachers and specialists involved in science education. These are not exhaustive or prescribed lists but rather a listing of possible suggestions that may help you modify your curriculum or instruc-

tion, based on the results of your probe, in order to help students learn ideas that they may be struggling with. It may be as simple as realizing that you need to provide a variety of contexts or that there may be a specific strategy or activity you could use with your students. Learning is a very complex process, and it is unlikely that any single suggestion will help all students learn the science ideas. But that is part of what formative assessment encourages—thinking carefully about a variety of instructional strategies and experiences. As you become more familiar with the ideas your students have and the multifaceted factors that may have contributed to their misunderstandings, you will identify additional strategies that you can use to teach for conceptual change.

## Related NSTA Science Store Publications and NSTA Journal Articles

The National Science Teachers Association's (NSTA) journals and books are increasingly targeting the ideas that students bring to their learning. For example, Bill Robertson's *Stop Faking It!* series of books may be helpful in clarifying content for students (as well as for teachers!). A journal article from one of NSTA's elementary, middle school, or high school journals may provide additional insight into students' misconceptions or provide an example of an effective instructional strategy or activity that can be used to develop understanding of the ideas targeted by a probe. To access the Science Store and journal articles, go to *www.nsta.org* and click on the appropriate site.

### Related Curriculum Topic Study Guides

NSTA is a co-publisher of the book *Science Curriculum Topic Study: Bridging the Gap Between Standards and Practice* (Keeley 2005). This book was developed as a professional development resource for teachers with funding from the National Science Foundation's Teacher Professional Continuum Program. It provides a set of 147 Curriculum Topic Study (CTS) guides that can be used to learn more about a science topic's content, examine instructional implications, identify specific learning goals and scientific ideas, examine the research on student learning, consider connections to other topics, examine the coherency of ideas that build over time, and link understandings to state and district standards. The CTS guides use national standards and research in a systematic process that deepens teachers' understanding of the topics they teach.

The probes in this book were developed using the CTS guides and the assessment tools and processes described in Chapter 4 of the CTS book. The CTS guides that were used to inform the development of each of the probes are listed in the teacher notes that follow each probe and can be used by teachers to extend those notes.

### References

References are provided for the standards and research findings cited in the teacher notes.

### Vignettes

The following three vignettes illustrate how a probe can be used in a variety of ways by teachers in elementary, middle, and high school. They show how teachers used the probes to elicit students' ideas before, during, and even after instruction for the purpose of informing their immediate teaching plans, adjusting instruction the next time they teach a unit, making curricular changes, or sharing their learning about students' ideas with their colleagues. The teachers in the vignettes are composites of teachers with whom the authors have worked.

### Elementary Vignette: Using the Probe "Is It an Animal?"

Before we began teaching our forest unit this year, the other third-grade teacher in my building and I decided to work on updating and revising the unit together. Both of us had taught this unit for several years and had gathered an enormous number of resources and teaching activities on the topic of "forests." Our elementary curriculum has a theme each year that draws on ideas from the state science standards about the diversity of life, ecology, structure and function, and how living things change over time. In first grade, students use butterflies as the context in which to learn ideas. In second grade, dinosaurs are the theme. Fourth graders use the theme of oceans to develop life science ideas.

We started by identifying goals for our students. We focused our first meeting on the goal of developing an understanding of

# Introduction

what distinguished animals from other organisms. This goal includes three performance indicators from our state (Maine Department of Education 1997):

- Design and describe a classification system for organisms.
- Describe the different living things within a given habitat.
- Compare and contrast the life cycles, behavior, and structure of different organisms.

Because we wanted to determine our students' level of knowledge and the kinds of prior experiences they would bring to the unit, we introduced the unit using the K-W-L strategy. This formative assessment strategy included asking what students knew about the topic, what they wanted to learn, and then, at the end of the unit, describing what they learned. Through this exercise we learned that students could name and describe a number of forest animals, but would certainly benefit from the activities we had designed in the upcoming weeks. We kept notes on our lessons as we worked through the unit and got together regularly to discuss the progress students were making. We found students sorted organisms in a variety of ways, including grouping organisms into plant and animal categories and forest and nonforest categories and by body coverings and motility strategies.

As a culminating activity, each student selected a forest animal to write a report on using information text and created a three-dimensional papier-mâché model of his or her chosen animal to put in the classroom "forest." Through these engaging experiences, our students learned a great deal about the forest and about the characteristics of the animals that live there. We had student "experts" on a variety of animals, including bears, deer, squirrels, owls, chipmunks, skunks, bobcats, wolves, raccoons, and even a lynx!

Later that year, my colleague and I attended a formative assessment conference where we learned about science assessment probes. We were encouraged to select a probe that we could try in our own classrooms. We were excited to discover the "Is It an Animal?" probe (Figure 3) because it fit so nicely with our forest unit. We took the probe back to school and immediately administered it to our third-grade students. Even though we had already taught the unit, we wanted to see if our instruction had made an impact on students' ability to retain the ideas they learned. Because some students in our class are English as a second language learners, we asked students to complete the first part of the probe independently after giving the directions and examples verbally and using pictures along with the examples. We then used an interview protocol for the second part, designed to capture students' thinking about why the pictures they circled were animals. We engaged the entire class in a discussion of the choices they made about animals and the reasons for their choices.

As we looked through the student papers and recalled the students' list of "rules" that emerged from the class discussion, we noted similarities in student thinking. The majority of students identified the cow, tiger, frog, snake, and monkey as animals. A little less than a quarter of the students identified the beetle, shark, snail, chicken, worm, and spider as animals, and an even fewer number of students recognized the boy or starfish as an animal. As a matter of fact, out of the 84 students we gave the probe to, only 9 identified the boy as an animal and 12 identified the worm! Even more revealing were the rules students gave in deciding whether or not something was an animal. These included the following:

- Animals have tails.
- Animals have fur and bones.
- Animals cannot walk on two feet.
- Animals have four or more legs.
- Animals can move by themselves.

Clearly our students had a limited view of animals. We reflected on what we could do differently in the future to better address and more fully develop the concept of "animal" with our third-grade students. We realized how helpful it would have been to have known the concepts our students held of animals before we developed the forest unit. We now know it is important to make certain that as students group organisms as animals they carefully examine the characteristics to see if they are truly exclusive. Which features do all animals have in common? Which features are different? Which characteristics of organisms are important to consider? Animals are more than warm, furry, four-legged creatures! Because so many students seemed

Figure 3  **Is It an Animal?**

Life, Earth, and Space Science Assessment **Probes**                    16

## Is It an Animal?

Which of the organisms listed are animals? Put an X next to each organism that is considered to be an animal.

| | |
|---|---|
| ___ cow | ___ spider |
| ___ tree | ___ snail |
| ___ mushroom | ___ flower |
| ___ human | ___ monkey |
| ___ worm | ___ beetle |
| ___ tiger | ___ whale |
| ___ shark | ___ frog      ___ mold |
| ___ starfish | ___ chicken   ___ snake |

Explain your thinking. Describe the "rule" or reasoning you used to decide if something is an animal.

_____
_____
_____
_____
_____
_____
_____
_____
_____
_____

Uncovering Student Ideas in Science                    117

# Introduction

to have a very narrow definition of *animal*, we need to diversify the organisms students come in contact with in our unit. We also realize we should give students real inquiry opportunities to observe and investigate real animals—not the papier-mâché variety.

Perhaps the most powerful learning from the experience of using a probe was the incredible depth of insight it provided to us as teachers. Using a probe that had been carefully designed to pull out some of the finer points and trouble spots based on cognitive research allowed us to "see" what was in the heads of our third graders, enabling us, in the future, to meet students where they were. The teacher notes that accompanied the assessment probe clearly indicated that we had overemphasized vertebrates, particularly mammals. We learned that the research shows that people have a limited understanding of the term *animal*.

Our intention in using the K-W-L strategy was to get information about the present thinking and understanding of third graders with respect to forests and animals. While this method did inform us of how students initially viewed the forest, it did not tell us all we needed to know about what students considered to be an animal. The forest was just a context for learning. A conception of "animal" was one of the ideas. We decided to have our students revisit their forest unit projects in the spring when we could go outside and visit a local woodland. We would design the experience to build on their prior learning, challenge their current ideas about what an animal is, and expand their classification of animals to include a variety of other

animals found in the forest, such as salamanders, millipedes, worms, birds, beetles, moths, toads, spiders, snakes, and even people.

The notion of using formative assessment probes to regularly "check in" on students' ideas has spurred us to use additional probes to gather information that will help us provide a more flexible and suitable pathway for students' learning. From now on our unit planning will always be informed by results from probes. In addition, we have shared our student data with the grade 4 teachers. As a result of seeing what our students struggled with, next year they are going to use a modified version of the same probe using ocean animals as part of their ocean unit, to see if the same students revert back to their preconceived ideas. As a result of what we found out, we will all be sure to develop the idea of what an animal is, using a variety of contexts and examples.

## Middle School Vignette: Using the Probe "Wet Jeans"

In sixth grade we study the water cycle. Our unit builds on experiences students had in elementary grades learning about change in state and developing an academic vocabulary to describe water when it changes state. When students come to sixth grade, they still remember the water cycle song they learned in third grade and don't hesitate to use words like *evaporation* and *condensation*.

This year I decided to use the "Wet Jeans" probe (Figure 4) before planning instruction that would include a review of concepts like evaporation and condensation. These seemed like fairly simple concepts that most of my students would probably remember and understand. Nevertheless, it would be helpful to find out if there were any students who still didn't understand evaporation so that I could design special instruction for them before moving on to the next set of ideas.

Wow! I wasn't prepared for the results! Instead of just a few students not understanding where water goes after it evaporates, most of the students in my class had major misconceptions! Even though they could comfortably use the word *evaporation,* over 75% of my students thought the water went immediately up to the Sun or the clouds. A few thought it no longer existed.

As I read through the teacher notes that came with the probe and examined my students' responses, it was clear to me that they used the word *evaporation* without understanding. Furthermore, it seems that they missed the grades 3–5 idea described in the related standards from *Benchmarks* that states, "When liquid water disappears, it turns into a

gas (vapor) in the air and can reappear as a liquid when cooled, or as a solid if cooled below the freezing point of water. Clouds and fog are made of tiny droplets of water" (AAAS 1993, p. 68). The research notes said students could understand this by fifth grade if they had received targeted instruction.

When I checked with the grades 3–5 teachers, they agreed that the idea of water existing in the air as water vapor was never explicitly

Figure 4 **Wet Jeans**

# Introduction

addressed. Students did know the water disappeared, but they didn't know where it actually went or what form it was in. This indicated to me that I needed to provide an opportunity for students to understand that the water is in the air around us. Then I could move on to the more complex idea of the global water cycle.

I decided to present my students with several everyday phenomena such as water droplets on the outside of a cold beverage glass, moisture on the bathroom window, and dew on the morning grass. I asked them to explain how the water got there, and they all answered "condensation and evaporation." However, when I pressed them to explain to me how the water actually got there, they had all sorts of interesting explanations. Only a few mentioned the water was in the air that came in contact with the object in question. I challenged students to think of a way they could prove where the water came from, and this led to a variety of interesting investigations. Eventually most students began to accept the idea that the water was in the air in a form they could not see. I also found this was an opportune time to tie the idea to conservation of matter so that students would understand that the water did not disappear in the sense that it no longer existed but rather it was just in a different form and different place.

Once my students could understand the meaning behind the terms *evaporation* and *condensation*, I would use these terms to discuss the processes that contribute to the water cycle. The teacher notes that came with the probe pointed out the flaws in water cycle diagrams. To see if my students continued to

accept the idea that water goes into the air initially before some of it travels upward to form clouds, I showed them a picture of the water cycle with an upward arrow pointing from a lake to a cloud. I asked them if that was a correct representation of evaporation. Most of my students pointed out that the diagram makes it look like water goes immediately up to a cloud, rather than existing in the surrounding air. I thought it was a good idea to have students discover this potential misrepresentation for themselves, as this is often the way the water cycle is illustrated in their textbooks.

I don't think I would have realized my students had this idea if I hadn't used the probe and combined my students' results with the readings that were in the probe teacher notes. It is quite possible that we would have covered the water cycle and my students would still believe that the water goes immediately up to the Sun or clouds. They would have passed a standardized assessment item asking them to label the process indicated by the upward arrow on a water cycle illustration and they would know the term, answer the test item correctly, yet still have misconceptions. Knowing the ideas they had about evaporation beforehand gave me an opportunity to design instruction to challenge their ideas and help my students develop a correct conception of where water goes after it evaporates and the form it takes.

## High School Vignette: Using the Probe "Is It Matter?"

This year, I have worked very hard to shift the focus of my chemistry strand in my ninth-grade, heterogeneously grouped integrated science class. One of my goals was to teach the concept of conservation of matter during chemical and physical changes. Understanding this concept will help students when they encounter stoichiometry as juniors in chemistry.

To start off my unit, I asked students to think about what might happen to the mass of solid or liquid matter as it underwent some sort of interaction (a physical or chemical change). After my students suggested a number of scenarios using solids and liquids, they developed and carried out a variety of investigations to test their ideas. Teams of students investigated materials that changed state, changed shape, dissolved, broke into separate pieces, or changed chemically. In general, students could accurately explain what happened to the mass in the experiments they carried out. Students developed a "rule" to explain their observations: "No matter what you do to the material, if nothing new is added or taken away, the mass will stay the same." This rule led to a formal definition of the conservation of matter.

After students had explored conservation of matter ideas in various contexts using solids and liquids, I decided to assess whether they would apply their present understandings to gases as well. I presented students with another scenario. I put an Alka-Seltzer tablet, flask of water, and an empty balloon on a scale. I asked students to predict what would happen to the total mass when the Alka-Seltzer tablet was placed in the flask of water and covered with a balloon. In the scenario it was explicitly stated that nothing could get in or out of the system. Surprisingly, when asked if matter would be con-

Figure 5 **Is It Matter?**

Physical Science Assessment **Probes** 10

## Is It Matter?

Listed below is a list of things that are considered matter and things that are not considered matter. Put an X next to each of the things that you consider to be matter.

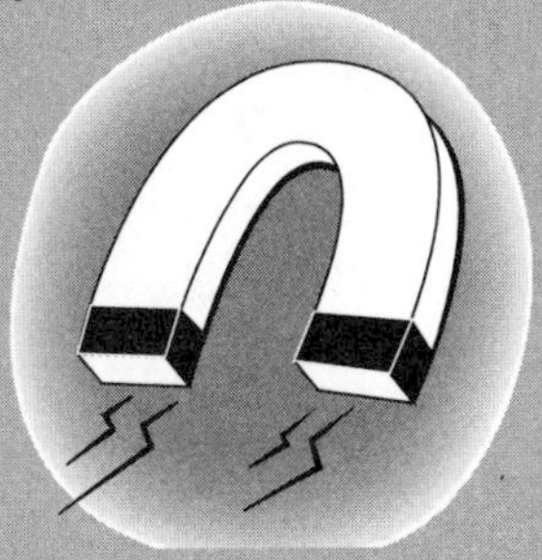

| | | | |
|---|---|---|---|
| ____ rocks | ____ salt | | |
| ____ baby powder | ____ Mars | | |
| ____ milk | ____ Jupiter | | |
| ____ air | ____ steam | | |
| ____ light | ____ rotten apples | | |
| ____ dust | ____ heat | | |
| ____ love | ____ sound waves | | |
| ____ cells | ____ water | | |
| ____ atoms | ____ bacteria | | |
| ____ fire | ____ oxygen | ____ gravity | ____ dissolved sugar |
| ____ smoke | ____ stars | ____ magnetic force | ____ electricity |

Explain your thinking. Describe the "rule" or reason you used to decide whether something is or is not matter.

______________________________

______________________________

______________________________

______________________________

______________________________

______________________________

______________________________

Uncovering Student Ideas in Science 79

# Introduction

served, a number of students said no because there was a gas in the balloon and gases don't weigh anything. Other students stated that the mass was not conserved because the tablet had dissolved into a powder that was weightless. I wondered where these ideas came from. Could my students be lacking a scientific conception of matter?

I decided to use a formative assessment probe to find out what my students' conception of matter was. I specifically wanted to find out what things they thought were matter and what things were not and what their "rule" was for defining matter. I gave them the probe in Figure 5.

I was quite surprised when I looked through the student work. Several students identified gravity, light, magnetic force, fire, and heat as matter while not marking air, cells, stars, dust, and dissolved sugar as matter. A number of students did not mark atoms as matter! What was going on here? Students listed several interesting reasons as their basis for classifying materials as matter or not matter, including that it has to be felt, it needs to be visible, it has to have weight, and the definition "matter is anything that has mass and occupies space." Yet they failed to recognize several forms of matter, such as air having mass, or they mistakenly identified forms of energy as having mass and volume. What was getting in the way of my students' understanding? Several students recalled a definition of *matter* but had difficulty applying it. If they didn't have a correct conception of matter, how could they apply conservation of matter ideas?

After reviewing the student work from the probe "Is It Matter?," I decided to investigate student thinking even further by observing students as they talked about their ideas with each other. The teacher notes that came with the probe described a method of card sorting that could give me additional information. I presented small groups of students with the items from the task on cards and asked them to sort them into two piles—a "matter" pile and "not matter" pile. This method allowed me to watch the faces of students as they worked through the exercise and discussed their ideas with their peers. Students hesitated when they were unclear or struggling with an example such as air, dissolved sugar, or sunlight. Occasionally, students would move cards as they reconsidered earlier choices, indicating uncertainty on their part.

Periodically, I asked students to explain why they had placed an item in a particular category and asked for elaboration when I wanted to explore a particular student's idea further. These observations and additional probing provided further evidence that my students were lacking a correct conception of matter. Furthermore, the research summaries described in the teacher notes confirmed what I was hearing from my students—in particular, the idea that gases do not have material character and thus are not considered matter.

I examined the suggestions for instruction and assessment provided in the teacher notes. I began to consider the contexts in which students had explored matter thus far and how these experiences might have influenced the patterns that were emerging in this set of student work. Had most of their experiences been with matter that they could see? How much experience had they had with gases? What kinds of experiences had they had in earlier grades with weighing and finding volumes? Were some of the items on the list more difficult for them to think about? Did they know what *mass* and *volume* mean? In which grade had they developed an operational definition of *matter*? It seemed as if the definition they were using was memorized without any understanding.

Despite the fact that I had revised my unit to more deliberately target conservation of matter ideas in a variety of contexts, I had missed a critical piece in my planning. Even though my students could express conservation of matter ideas and conserve matter in a number of situations, they would not be able to fully comprehend the idea of conservation of matter without a clear understanding of what matter is. I had been using the term *matter* throughout the unit assuming that students had this prerequisite knowledge. The word *matter* is everywhere! In prior grades we refer to "properties of matter," "changes in matter," and "states of matter," but we fail to first help students develop a conception of what constitutes matter. Even though we were investigating forms of matter and conserving matter, I found it was worth taking the time to make sure that my students have a conception of what matter is. I will change my activities to explicitly address and challenge my students' conception of matter, particularly regarding gases and dissolved substances.

## Concept Matrices and Probe Set

The remainder of this book contains a set of 25 probes that you can use with your students along with accompanying teacher notes for each probe. The concept matrices (p. 24 and 116) indicate the concepts most related to each probe and can be used to select probes that match your instructional context. In this volume we focus on the following topics: forms of matter; changes in matter; light, heat, and sound energy; living things and life processes; cells; weathering and erosion; phases of the moon; and gravity. Later volumes will include additional topics in life, Earth, space, and physical science.

## References

American Association for the Advancement of Science (AAAS). 1993. *Benchmarks for science literacy*. New York: Oxford University Press.

Atkin, J. M., and J. E. Coffey, eds. 2003. *Everyday assessment in the science classroom*. Arlington, VA: NSTA Press.

Black, P., C. Harrison, C. Lee, B. Marshall, and D. Wiliam. 2003. *Assessment for learning: Putting it into practice*. Berkshire, England: Open University Press.

Bransford, J. D., A. L. Brown, and R. R. Cocking, eds. 1999. *How people learn: Brain, mind, experience, and school*. Washington, DC: National Academy Press.

Donovan, M. S., and J. Bransford. 2005.

# Introduction

*How students learn science in the classroom.* Washington, DC: National Academy Press.

Driver, R., A. Squires, P. Rushworth, and V. Wood-Robinson. 1994. *Making sense of secondary science: Research into children's ideas.* London and New York: RoutledgeFalmer.

Keeley, P. 2005. *Science curriculum topic study: Bridging the gap between standards and practice.* Thousand Oaks, CA: Corwin Press.

Maine Department of Education. 1997. *Maine's learning results.* Augusta, ME: Maine State Government Printing Office.

Minstrell, J., and E. van Zee. 2003. Using questioning to assess and foster student thinking. In *Everyday assessment in the science classroom*, eds. J. M. Atkin and J. E. Coffey, 61–73. Arlington, VA: NSTA Press.

National Research Council (NRC). 1996. *National science education standards.* Washington, DC: National Academy Press.

Pelligrino, J., N. Chudowksy, and R. Glaser. 2001. *Knowing what students know: The science and design of educational assessment.* Washington, DC: National Academy Press.

Sneider, C. 2003. Examining students' work. In *Everyday assessment in the science classroom,* eds. J. M. Atkin and J. E. Coffey, 27–40. Arlington, VA: NSTA Press.

Stavy, R., and D. Tirosh. 2000. *How students (mis-) understand science and mathematics: Intuitive rules.* New York: Teachers College Press.

# Physical Science Assessment Probes

**Physical Science Assessment Probes**
Concept Matrix

# Probes

| Core Science Concepts | Light | | | Sound | Matter | | | | | | | | Gravity | Heat and Temperature | |
|---|---|---|---|---|---|---|---|---|---|---|---|---|---|---|---|
| | Can It Reflect Light? | Apple in the Dark | Birthday Candles | Making Sound | Ice Cubes in a Bag | Lemonade | Cookie Crumbles | Seedlings in a Jar | Is It Melting? | Is It Matter? | Is It Made of Molecules? | The Rusty Nails | Talking About Gravity | The Mitten Problem | Objects and Temperature |
| Conservation of Matter | | | | | ✓ | ✓ | ✓ | ✓ | | | | | | | |
| Mass or Weight | | | | | ✓ | ✓ | ✓ | ✓ | | ✓ | | ✓ | | | |
| Atoms or Molecules | | | | | ✓ | | | ✓ | | ✓ | ✓ | | | | |
| Dissolving | | | | | | ✓ | | | ✓ | | | | | | |
| States of Matter | | | | | | | | | ✓ | | | | | | |
| Change in State | | | | | ✓ | | | | ✓ | | | | | | |
| Physical Change | | | | | ✓ | ✓ | ✓ | | ✓ | | | | | | |
| Chemical Change | | | | | | | | ✓ | | | | ✓ | | | |
| Oxidation | | | | | | | | | | | | ✓ | | | |
| Concept of Matter | | | | | | | | | | ✓ | ✓ | | | | |
| Melting | | | | | | | | | ✓ | | | | | | |
| Closed System | | | | | ✓ | | | ✓ | | | | | | | |
| Light | ✓ | ✓ | ✓ | | | | | | | | | | | | |
| Reflection | ✓ | ✓ | | | | | | | | | | | | | |
| Light Transmission | | ✓ | ✓ | | | | | | | | | | | | |
| Color | | ✓ | | | | | | | | | | | | | |
| Vision | | ✓ | ✓ | | | | | | | | | | | | |
| Light Source | | | ✓ | | | | | | | | | | | | |
| Sound | | | | ✓ | | | | | | | | | | | |
| Vibration | | | | ✓ | | | | | | | | | | | |
| Heat | | | | | | | | | ✓ | | | | | ✓ | ✓ |
| Temperature | | | | | | | | | | | | | | ✓ | ✓ |
| Energy | | | | | | | | | | | | | | ✓ | |
| Gravity | | | | | | | | | | | | | ✓ | ✓ | |

# Can It Reflect Light?

What types of objects or materials can reflect light? Put an X next to the things you think can reflect light.

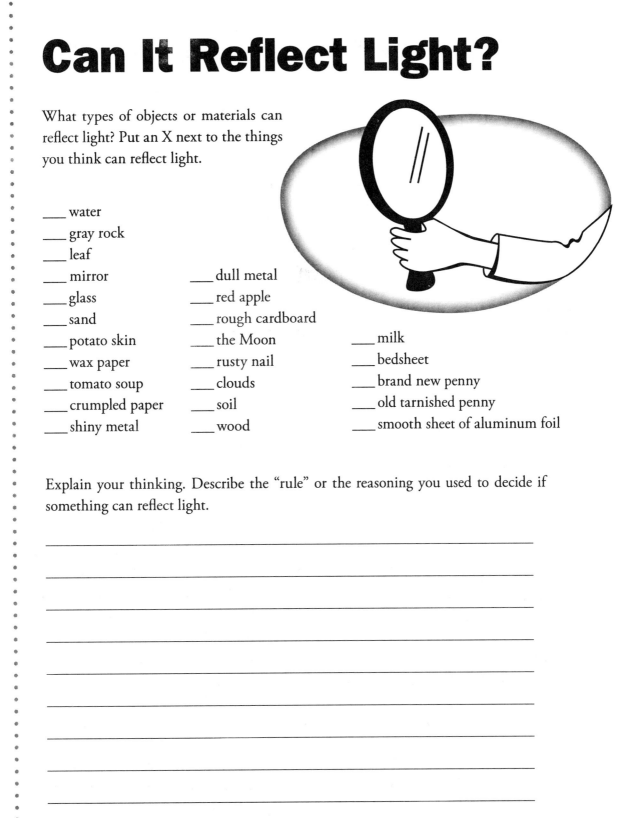

___ water

___ gray rock

___ leaf

___ mirror      ___ dull metal

___ glass      ___ red apple

___ sand      ___ rough cardboard

___ potato skin      ___ the Moon      ___ milk

___ wax paper      ___ rusty nail      ___ bedsheet

___ tomato soup      ___ clouds      ___ brand new penny

___ crumpled paper      ___ soil      ___ old tarnished penny

___ shiny metal      ___ wood      ___ smooth sheet of aluminum foil

Explain your thinking. Describe the "rule" or the reasoning you used to decide if something can reflect light.

_____

_____

_____

_____

_____

_____

_____

_____

_____

# Can It Reflect Light?

## Teacher Notes

## Purpose

The purpose of this assessment probe is to elicit students' ideas about light reflection off ordinary objects and materials. The probe is designed to find out if students recognize that all non-light-emitting objects that we can see reflect some light or if they believe that only certain types of objects reflect light.

## Related Concepts

light, reflection

## Explanation

Assuming all of the objects on the list are visible to an observer, the best response is "All of the objects on the list can reflect light." The objects and materials on this list can be seen when light is reflected from the object or material and enters the eye. When we can see a nonluminous object, we know that some or all of the light striking the object is reflected to our eye. Otherwise we would not be able to see it. Most materials will absorb some wavelengths of light and reflect the rest. This accounts for why we see different colors. When we see white, all colors have been reflected back. Materials that absorb all light and reflect no light appear black. Black is the absence of light. Black objects whose features you can actually see do not absorb all the light that falls on them. With these objects, some reflection at the surface allows you to see their features. Some materials clearly reflect light better than others. Ordinary mirrors and light, shiny, smooth objects reflect light to the observer because the light bounces off the surface at a definite angle. When light hits rough surfaces, such as paper or rock, it is scattered and bounces back in many different directions. This scattering makes some objects appear dull.

## Curricular and Instructional Considerations

### Elementary Students

Knowing that light can be reflected, refracted, or absorbed when it comes in contact with an object or material is a grade-level expectation in the national standards. Students at this age engage in learning opportunities that involve examining the properties of a variety of objects and materials. The probe is useful at this grade level for examining how students connect their ideas about certain observable properties of objects and materials to ideas about reflection of light. It is important for students to develop the generalization that all visible objects reflect some amount of light, an important prerequisite to understanding how vision works (a topic that is traditionally studied in middle school).

### Middle School Students

Students develop an understanding that nonluminous objects are seen as a result of light being reflected off the object and entering the eye. This idea is a grade-level expectation in the national standards. However, they often fail to recognize the closely linked idea that if you can see something, then it must be reflecting light. This notion explains why each of the visible objects on the list reflect some light. Middle school students typically engage in learning activities that examine the directionality and angle of light as it passes through

or reflects off objects. They frequently engage in activities that use mirrors. They use ideas about reflection and absorption to explain how colors are seen. At this level the probe is useful in determining whether students are "context-bound" in their thinking or if they are making the generalization that an object, regardless of the type of material or color, is reflecting some light if it is seen by the eye.

### High School Students

Students develop more sophisticated ideas about light reflection and optics. They may, however, still be context-bound or persist in their intuitive notions that certain characteristics of objects, such as dull or bumpy surfaces, inhibit light reflection. The notion of light reflection by ordinary objects is fundamental to optics instruction and is used to understand image processes such as photography.

### Administering the Probe

Be sure students are familiar with the objects on the list. Ask them to cross out any word or object they are unfamiliar with. You might consider explaining, or showing an example of, an object if students are not sure what it is. This probe can also be used as a card sort. In small groups, students can sort cards listing each item into two groups—those that reflect light and those that do not reflect light. Listening carefully to students' discussions with each other as they sort can lend insight into their thinking. This probe can be combined with "Apple in

Topic: Light
Go to: *www.scilinks.org*
Code: USIS27

the Dark" to further examine students' ideas about the role of light.

## Related Ideas in *National Science Education Standards* (NRC 1996)

### K–4 Properties of Objects and Materials

• Objects have many observable properties.

### K–4 Light, Heat, Electricity, and Magnetism

★ Light can be reflected by a mirror, refracted by a lens, or absorbed by an object.

### 5–8 Transfer of Energy

★ Light interacts with matter by transmission (including refraction), absorption, or scattering (including reflection). For a person to see an object, light from that object—emitted by or scattered from it— must enter the eye.

## Related Ideas in *Benchmarks for Science Literacy* (AAAS 1993)

### K–2 Structure of Matter

• Objects can be described in terms of their physical properties (color, texture, etc.)

### 3–5 Motion (New benchmark from "Waves" map in *Atlas of Science Literacy* [AAAS 2001])

★ Light travels and tends to maintain its direction of motion until it interacts with an object or material. Light can be absorbed, redirected, bounced back, or allowed to pass through.

### 6–8 Motion

• Light from the Sun is made up of a mixture of many different colors of light, even though to the eye the light looks almost white. Other things that give off or reflect light have a different mix of colors.

• Something can be "seen" when light waves emitted or reflected by it enter the eye.

## Related Research

• Studies by Guesne (1985) and Ramadas and Driver (1989) revealed that middle school students will accept the idea that mirrors reflect light but may not accept the idea that ordinary objects reflect light (AAAS 1993).

• Students' ideas about reflection may be context-bound. Many students questioned in a study conducted by Anderson and Smith (1983) could describe light as bouncing off mirrors but not off other objects. A few students even lacked a conception of light bouncing or reflecting off any objects. The researchers also found that 61% of the children they sampled thought color to be a property of an object rather than reflected light off an object (Driver et al. 1994).

## Suggestions for Instruction and Assessment

• By experimenting with light, K–4 students begin to understand that phenomena can be observed, measured, and controlled in various ways (NRC 1996).

---

★ Indicates a strong match between the ideas elicited by the probe and a national standard's learning goal.

- "Light can be reflected by a mirror, refracted by a lens, or absorbed by an object" is a learning goal in the National Science Education Standards (NRC 1996). However, use caution when addressing this standard as it may imply to some students and teachers that only mirrors reflect light if other examples are not included. Provide students with a variety of materials to investigate reflection. There is a danger of students becoming context-bound if their experiences only include mirrors or shiny and smooth objects. Emphasize the generalization rather than focusing exclusively on one type of object.

- Explicitly link the idea that if we can see an object, regardless of its observable physical properties, it is reflecting or emitting some light in order for us to be able to see it.

- Have students use a flashlight to observe light reflecting off smooth aluminum foil and rough aluminum foil. Connect this experience with an analogy of a ball (representing the light) bouncing on a smooth floor versus a bumpy surface. Take students outside to bounce a ball on a smooth pavement and then compare how the ball bounces on gravel or some other rough surface. Connect the idea to what happens to light on smooth and rough surfaces (see Matkins and McDonnough [2004] under "Related NSTA Science Store Publications and NSTA Journal Articles," below).

- Use real-life applications, such as remote-sensing images, to develop the idea that

Earth materials such as water, vegetation, rocks, soil, sand, and clouds reflect light that is detected by satellites.

- Ask students to draw and explain ray diagrams that compare light reflecting off smooth versus rough objects.

- Identify various physical properties of materials and their associated vocabulary, such as *texture, luster, color, transparency, translucence,* and *opaqueness* and compare and contrast what happens when light interacts with these materials.

- Alert students to the ways our English language refers to reflection, such as *reflection pools* and *seeing our reflection* in a mirror or shiny object. Reflection is almost always spoken of in the context of mirrors, shiny objects, and water. Objects and materials like paper, wood, soil, and rocks are seldom referred to as reflective materials.

- Modify the assessment probe by having students come up with their own list of things they think reflect light and things that do not reflect light. Have them use their own list to explain their reasons for deciding whether an object or material reflects light.

## Related NSTA Science Store Publications and NSTA Journal Articles

American Association for the Advancement of Science (AAAS). 1993. *Benchmarks for science literacy.* New York: Oxford University Press.

American Association for the Advancement of Science (AAAS). 2001. *Atlas of science literacy.* (See

"Waves," pp. 64–65.) New York: Oxford University Press.

Driver, R., A. Squires, P. Rushworth, and V. Wood-Robinson. 1994. *Making sense of secondary science: Research into children's ideas.* London and New York: RoutledgeFalmer.

Keeley, P. 2005. *Science curriculum topic study: Bridging the gap between standards and practice.* Thousand Oaks, CA: Corwin Press.

Magnusson, S., and S. Palincsar. 2005. Teaching to promote the development of scientific knowledge and reasoning about light at the elementary school level. In *How students learn: Science in the classroom,* eds. M. S. Donovan and J. Bransford. Washington, DC: National Academy Press.

Matkins, J., and J. McDonnough. 2004. Circus of light. *Science and Children* (Feb.): 50–54.

Robertson, W. 2003. *Light: Stop faking it! Finally understanding science so you can teach it.* Arlington, VA: NSTA Press.

Stepans, J. 2003. *Targeting students' science misconceptions: Physical science concepts using the conceptual change model.* (See section on light and color.) Tampa, FL: Showboard.

**Related Curriculum Topic Study Guides**
(Keeley 2005)
"Visible Light, Color, and Vision"
"Senses"

## References

American Association for the Advancement of Science (AAAS). 1993. *Benchmarks for science literacy.* New York: Oxford University Press.

American Association for the Advancement of Science (AAAS). 2001. *Atlas of science literacy.* New York: Oxford University Press.

Anderson, C., and E. Smith. 1983. Children's conceptions of light and color: Developing the concepts of unseen rays. Paper presented to the annual meeting of the American Educational Research Association, Montreal, Canada.

Driver, R., A. Squires, P. Rushworth, and V. Wood-Robinson. 1994. *Making sense of secondary science: Research into children's ideas.* London and New York: RoutledgeFalmer.

Guesne, E. 1985. Light. In *Children's ideas in science,* eds. R. Driver, E. Guesne, and A. Tiberghien, 10–32. Milton Keynes, UK: Open University Press.

Keeley, P. 2005. *Science curriculum topic study: Bridging the gap between standards and practice.* Thousand Oaks, CA: Corwin Press.

National Research Council (NRC). 1996. *National science education standards.* Washington DC: National Academy Press.

Ramadas, J., and R. Driver. 1989. *Aspects of secondary students' ideas about light.* Leeds, UK: University of Leeds Centre for Studies in Science and Mathematics Education.

# Apple in the Dark

Imagine you are sitting at a table with a red apple in front of you. Your friend closes the door and turns off all the lights. It is totally dark in the room. There are no windows in the room or cracks around the door. No light can enter the room.

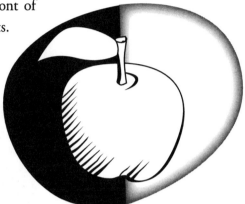

Circle the statement you believe best describes how you would see the apple in the dark:

**A**  You will not see the red apple, regardless of how long you are in the room.

**B**  You will see the red apple after your eyes have had time to adjust to the darkness.

**C**  You will see the apple after your eyes have had time to adjust to the darkness, but you will not see the red color.

**D**  You will see only the shadow of the apple after your eyes have had time to adjust to the darkness.

**E**  You will see only a faint outline of the apple after your eyes have had time to adjust to the darkness.

Describe your thinking. Provide an explanation for your answer.

_____

_____

_____

_____

_____

_____

_____

_____

_____

# Apple in the Dark

## Teacher Notes

## Purpose

The purpose of this assessment probe is to elicit students' ideas about how we see objects. The probe is designed to find out if students know that light must be reflected off an object and enter the eye in order for a non-light-emitting object to be visible. The probe helps teachers identify various conceptual models students use to link the role of light to vision.

## Related Concepts

light, light reflection, light transmission, color, vision

## Explanation

The best response is A. In order to see an object, light must be emitted from or reflected off an object so that it reaches the eye. The path of light is from the object to the eye. It is impossible to see an object in the absence of light (total darkness). However, it is important to be aware that choosing the correct response and explaining that light is needed is not sufficient evidence that students understand that emitted or reflected light must enter the eye in order to see an object. They may simply think that an object is illuminated by light in the room or the eye is the activator of vision when light is present.

## Curricular and Instructional Considerations

### Elementary Students

Students are beginning to develop ideas about light as something that travels from its source and strikes objects. They begin to recognize that some objects, like a lightbulb, give off their own light and others reflect light. While they may begin to develop an understanding that light travels and is reflected off objects, they have difficulty connecting this idea to how we see. They use various conceptual models that include or do not include light reflection to explain how objects are seen. This probe is useful for finding out elementary students' beginning ideas about light and color and about darkness as the absence of light. It also determines whether students are starting to make a connection between light and how we see.

## Middle School Students

Students begin to connect the idea that light reflects off an object to their understanding of how vision works. Knowing that objects become visible when the light emitted or reflected by them enters the eye is a grade-level expectation in the national standards. This probe is useful for identifying middle school students' prior conceptions before designing instruction explicitly aimed at the connection between light and vision.

## High School Students

At this level the probe is useful for identifying the middle school prerequisite ideas prior to more sophisticated light and optics instruction in high school. Examining students' responses to this probe can help physics or physical science teachers determine whether students retain alternative ideas about "seeing in the dark" even years after formal concept development in middle school.

## Administering the Probe

Make sure students understand there is no light in the room. Although this is explicitly stated in the probe, some students may assume there is some light present because the experience of total darkness is unfamiliar to many.

## Related Ideas in *National Science Education Standards* (NRC 1996)

. . . . . . . . . . . . . . . . . . . . . . . . . . . .

### K–4 Light, Heat, Electricity, and Magnetism

- Light travels in a straight line until it strikes an object.

### 5–8 Transfer of Energy

★ Light interacts with matter by transmission. To see an object, light from that object—emitted or scattered from it—must enter the eye.

## Related Ideas in *Benchmarks for Science Literacy* (AAAS 1993)

. . . . . . . . . . . . . . . . . . . . . . . . . . . .

### 3–5 Motion (New benchmark from "Waves" map in *Atlas of Science Literacy* [AAAS 2001])

- Light travels and tends to maintain its direction of motion until it interacts with an object or material. Light can be absorbed, redirected, bounced back, or allowed to pass through.

### 6–8 Motion

★ Something can be "seen" when light waves

★ Indicates a strong match between the ideas elicited by the probe and a national standard's learning goal.

emitted or reflected by it enter the eye.

## Related Research

- Several studies have shown that students of all ages have difficulty understanding that light must enter the eye in order to see an object. Elementary and middle school students who do not understand that light is something that travels away from its source to another place have difficulty explaining reflection of light off objects (AAAS 1993).
- A variety of alternative conceptual models used by students have been identified to explain the role or absence of light in explaining vision (Driver et al. 1994).
- Ramadas and Driver (1989) asked 456 high school students to explain what happens between a book and the eyes of a girl who is reading the book. Only 31% of the students were able to describe a correct model of light reflection and vision. This was combined with a similar study conducted by Andersson and Karrqvist (1983) of 12- to 15-year-olds who revealed various alternative ideas, including simply that light helps us see better, the eye is the activator of vision rather than the receiver, something goes from the eye to the book, something goes back and forth between the eye and the book, light illuminates an object so we can see it, and a contrast with dark helps us to see.
- Ramadas and Driver (1989; see Driver et al. 1994) reported that "many children did not recognize the necessity of light for vision and thought it was possible to see

when it was dark. Having not experienced total darkness, they did not appreciate that light must be present in a room if they could see objects, however faintly" (p. 42).
- The idea that the eye can see without anything linking it to an object is a persistent notion that exists even after students have had traditional instruction in optics (Guesne 1985).
- Fetherstonhaugh and Treagust (1990) investigated students' ideas about seeing in the dark. They found a significant number of children believe that people can see in the dark and that this was more prevalent among city dwellers than children who live in rural areas. However, in both groups of children, over 40% believe that cats can see in total darkness.
- The Annenberg/CPB Private Universe Project (1995) conducted interviews with students in the dark to find out if they believed they would see an object and its color in total darkness. The students interviewed held persistently to the idea that if they waited long enough, they would eventually see the object.

## Suggestions for Instruction and Assessment

- The National Science Education Standards (NRC 1996) encourage investigation by elementary students so that they may begin to understand that phenomena can be observed, measured, and controlled in various ways. Phenomena that provide observational evidence for light traveling from a source and reflection should begin to be investigated in elementary grades.

- Most students have never experienced total darkness. Even in a dark room or outside, there is some light diffusing or reflected from a source that allows students to see faint images. Having students experience total darkness in a sealed-off room, photographic darkroom, or dark box may be helpful. Also, ask students to think of areas where there would be total darkness (e.g., in a mine shaft or deep within a cave).

- The ideas in this task can be tested by students in school or at home. After students commit to an outcome, have them test it with an apple in a darkened, windowless room, closet, or dark box. Encourage students to think about their observations, and discuss reasons that could explain why their experience did not match their prediction. Students may come up with the correct explanation on their own through a dissonance-resolving discussion.

- Combine learning about the nature of light with the nature of vision. Explicitly link how light travels from an emitting source or reflection off an object with how we see objects. Students may understand how light reflects in straight lines, refracts, and scatters but may still fail to link these concepts to how we see objects unless it is addressed in instruction.

- Use a variety of contexts. Students may understand the idea of direction of reflection of

light and how it enters the eye when working with mirrors or shiny surfaces but may fail to apply ideas to light sources, ordinary objects like an apple, or dull surfaces.

- Be aware that activities such as observing pupils of the eye getting larger in the dark and learning about nocturnal animals with large eyes may contribute to the idea that it is the eye alone that is responsible for seeing. Emphasize that these biological features are intended to maximize the amount of light that can enter the eye.

- Encourage students to draw directional diagrams that include a light source, an object, and the eye to show how the eye sees an object. Ask students to explain their diagrams.

- Modify the assessment to contrast ideas about black, white, and different-colored objects.

## Related NSTA Science Store Publications and NSTA Journal Articles

American Association for the Advancement of Science (AAAS). 2001. *Atlas of science literacy.* (See "Waves," p. 65.) New York: Oxford University Press.

Driver, R., A. Squires, P. Rushworth, and V. Wood-Robinson. 1994. *Making sense of secondary science: Research into children's ideas.* London and New York: RoutledgeFalmer.

Keeley, P. 2005. *Science curriculum topic study: Bridging the gap between standards and practice.* Thousand Oaks, CA: Corwin Press.

Matkins, J., and J. McDonnough. 2004. Circus of

light. *Science and Children* (Feb.): 50–54.

Robertson, W. 2003. *Light: Stop faking it! Finally understanding science so you can teach it.* Arlington, VA: NSTA Press.

Stepans, J. 2003. *Targeting students' science misconceptions: Physical science concepts using the conceptual change model.* (See section on light and color.) Tampa, FL: Showboard.

**Related Curriculum Topic Study Guides**
(Keeley 2005)
"Visible Light, Color, and Vision"
"Senses"

## References

American Association for the Advancement of Science (AAAS). 1993. *Benchmarks for science literacy.* New York: Oxford University Press.

American Association for the Advancement of Science (AAAS). 2001. *Atlas of science literacy.* New York: Oxford University Press.

Andersson, B., and C. Karrqvist. 1983. How Swedish pupils aged 12–15 years understand light and its properties. *European Journal of Science Education* 5 (4): 387–402.

Driver, R., A. Squires, P. Rushworth, and V. Wood-Robinson. 1994. *Making sense of secondary science: Research into children's ideas.* London and New York: RoutledgeFalmer.

Fetherstonhaugh, T., and D. F. Treagust. 1990. Students' understanding of light and its properties following a teaching strategy to engender conceptual change. Paper presented at the annual meeting of the American Educational Research Association, Boston.

Guesne, E. 1985. Light. In *Children's ideas in science,* eds. R. Driver, E. Guesne, and A. Tiberghien, 10–32. Milton Keynes, UK: Open University Press.

National Research Council (NRC). 1996. *National science education standards.* Washington, DC: National Academy Press.

Private Universe Project. 1995. *The Private Universe Teacher Workshop Series.* [Videotape] South Burlington, VT: The Annenberg/CPB Math and Science Collection.

Ramadas, J., and R. Driver. 1989. *Aspects of secondary students' ideas about light.* Leeds, UK: University of Leeds Centre for Studies in Science and Mathematics Education.

# Birthday Candles

Imagine you are at a birthday party. A birthday cake with candles is put on a table in the middle of a room. The room is very large. You are standing at the end of the room, 10 meters away from the cake. You can see the candles. Circle the reponse that best describes how far the light from the candles traveled in order for you to see the flames.

**A** The light stays on the candle flames.

**B** The light travels a few centimeters from the candle flames.

**C** The light travels about 1 meter.

**D** The light travels about halfway to where you are standing.

**E** The light travels all the way to where you are standing.

Describe your thinking. Provide an explanation for your answer.

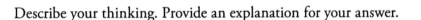
_____

_____

_____

_____

_____

_____

_____

_____

_____

_____

# Birthday Candles

## Teacher Notes

## Purpose

The purpose of this assessment probe is to elicit students' ideas about how light travels outward from its source. The probe is designed to find out if students recognize that light will travel outward from its source, generally in a straight line regardless of distance, until it comes in contact with matter that may change its direction. It also helps determine if students recognize there is light in the space between the visible part of an object that they can clearly detect (the flame) and their eyes.

## Related Concepts

light, light source, light transmission, vision

## Explanation

The best response is E. The light from the candles will travel away from its source (the flame) to you as long as it is unobstructed by an object or material. Since you can see the candlelight, it has traveled outward from its source—the candle flame—through the room and to your eyes. For you to see the flame, the light emitted from the flame must reach your eye. The eyes are the object, or matter, that the light comes in contact with. Even though it may appear to the student in a lit room that there is only light around the candle, since that is what they can detect with their senses, light is radiating outward in all directions beyond the visible part of the flame, including the space between the light source and the eye of the observer.

## Curricular and Instructional Considerations

Topic: Using Light
Go to: *www.scilinks.org*
Code: USIS39

### Elementary Students

Students are beginning to develop early ideas about light as "straight lines or rays" that travel from their source until they contact an object or material. Knowing that light keeps moving in a straight line until it strikes an object is a grade-level expectation in the national standards. Students at this level begin to recognize that some objects, like a candle flame, give off their own light that radiates outward in all directions. While they may start to understand that light travels outward from its source, they may have difficulty conceptualizing that the light travels further than the actual light effect they can see. They may have various conceptual models that include light illuminating a limited space around its source. Their observations of the light surrounding a candle flame may limit their thinking about how far the light travels. This probe is useful in eliciting preconceptions that develop early on.

### Middle School Students

When students begin middle school they should know that light keeps traveling in a given direction until it interacts with a material or object. Knowing that in order to see a luminous object, light emitted from a source (in this case the candle) must enter the eye is a grade-level expectation in the national standards. This probe is useful in determining whether students recognize that light exists between the source and the observer and continues to travel beyond the visible light seen around the candle flames to the eye of the observer. Combining these two ideas is slightly

more sophisticated than the elementary notion that light travels outward until it strikes an object. This probe is useful in determining whether early preconceptions still persist after elementary grades instruction.

### High School Students

At the high school level this probe is useful for identifying prerequisite ideas prior to light and optics instruction. It can be used to determine whether students still revert to their early preconceptions about light transmission held in earlier grades, even after formal concept development in middle school.

### Administering the Probe

This probe scenario may be modeled with students. Have students stand around the outside of a room. Place a candle in the center of the room where all students can see it, have students observe the flame, and then pose the question. (*Safety note:* Use a candle wider than it is tall and have an ABC fire extinguisher at hand.)

## Related Ideas in *National Science Education Standards* (NRC 1996)

. . . . . . . . . . . . . . . . . . . . . . . . . . . .

### K–4 Light, Heat, Electricity, and Magnetism

★ Light travels in a straight line until it strikes an object.

### 5–8 Transfer of Energy

★ Light interacts with matter by transmission.

---

★ Indicates a strong match between the ideas elicited by the probe and a national standard's learning goal.

To see an object, light from that object—emitted or scattered from it—must enter the eye.

## Related Ideas in *Benchmarks for Science Literacy* (AAAS 1993)

### 3–5 Motion (New benchmark from "Waves" map in *Atlas of Scientific Literacy* [AAAS 2001])

★ Light travels and tends to maintain its direction of motion until it interacts with an object or material.

### 6–8 Motion

★ Something can be "seen" when light waves emitted or reflected by it enter the eye.

## Related Research

- Studies of 10- and 11-year-old students show that they fail to recognize light as an entity that exists between its source and its effect. They fail to recognize light as something that travels. Two different conceptions of light exist among students that age: (1) light equated with a source and (2) light as an entity located in the space between its source and effect (Guesne 1985).

- The fact that the path that light takes is not directly visible results in comprehension difficulties for students (Ramadas and Driver 1989).

- A study conducted by Stead and Osborne (1980) used the context of a candle in the daytime and found that students did not think light traveled very far from its source.

- Students' reasoning about how far light travels may be related to intuitive rules described by Stavy and Tirosh (1995) in which more A equals more B. In other words, a more intense light (than a candle flame) results in a greater distance traveled.

## Suggestions for Instruction and Assessment

- By experimenting with light, K–4 students begin to understand that phenomena can be observed, measured, and controlled in various ways (NRC 1996).

- Explicitly address the idea that light exists in the space between where we see its effect and its source, even though we may not be able to see it directly.

- Middle and high school students can use examples of sources that are very far away, such as the Sun, to explore the idea that light is in the space between its source and where we receive it.

- Project light from a flashlight or other projection device in a lit room. Have students think about ways to test whether there is light between the source and its projection on the wall. Students cannot see the light in between, but, when they hold their hand or a piece of paper in the path of the light, they see that the light projects on it. This phenomenon can help develop the idea that light is traveling in the space between the source and its observable effect.

- Use additional assessments with other examples besides the candle. Children may use a variety of prior ideas depending on

---

★ Indicates a strong match between the ideas elicited by the probe and a national standard's learning goal.

what the situation is, so it is difficult to ascertain their conceptual model based on one instance. Consider changing the context to a campfire, a lightbulb, a Halloween light stick, etc., and vary the conditions to include both night and day.

## Related NSTA Science Store Publications and NSTA Journal Articles

American Association for the Advancement of Science (AAAS). 2001. *Atlas of science literacy.* (See "Waves," pp. 64–65.) New York: Oxford University Press.

Keeley, P. 2005. *Science curriculum topic study: Bridging the gap between standards and practice.* Thousand Oaks, CA: Corwin Press.

Robertson, W. 2003. *Light: Stop faking it! Finally understanding science so you can teach it.* Arlington, VA: NSTA Press.

Stavy, R., and D. Tirosh. 1995. *How students (mis-) understand science and mathematics: Intuitive rules.* New York: Teachers College Press.

Stepans, J. 2003. *Targeting students' science misconceptions: Physical science concepts using the conceptual change model.* (See section on light and color.) Tampa, FL: Showboard.

**Related Curriculum Topic Study Guide**
(Keeley 2005)
"Visible Light, Color, and Vision"

## References

American Association for the Advancement of Science (AAAS). 1993. *Benchmarks for science literacy.* New York: Oxford University Press.

American Association for the Advancement of Science (AAAS). 2001. *Atlas of science literacy.* New York: Oxford University Press

Guesne, E. 1985. Light. In *Children's ideas in science,* eds. R. Driver, E. Guesne, and A. Tiberghien, 10–22. Milton Keynes, UK: Open University Press.

Keeley, P. 2005. *Science curriculum topic study: Bridging the gap between standards and practice.* Thousand Oaks, CA: Corwin Press.

National Research Council (NRC). 1996. *National science education standards.* Washington, DC: National Academy Press.

Ramadas, J., and R. Driver. 1989. *Aspects of secondary students' ideas about light.* Leeds, UK: University of Leeds Centre for Studies in Science and Mathematics Education.

Stavy, R., and D. Tirosh. 1995. *How students (mis-) understand science and mathematics: Intuitive rules.* New York: Teachers College Press.

Stead, B., and R. Osborne. 1980. Exploring students' concepts of light. *The Australian Science Teacher's Journal* 26 (3): 84–90.

# Making Sound

All of the objects listed below make sounds. Put an X next to the objects you think involve vibrations in producing sound.

____ guitar strings

____ drum

____ dripping faucet

____ barking dog

____ piano

____ screeching brakes

____ radio speaker     ____ drum

____ crumpled paper     ____ wind         ____ hammer

____ car engine         ____ wood saw     ____ flute

____ chirping cricket     ____ clapped hands     ____ thunderstorm

____ singer           ____ bubbling water     ____ two stones rubbed together

____ popped balloon     ____ rustling leaves     ____ snapped fingers

Explain your thinking. What "rule" or reasoning did you use to decide which objects involve vibrations in producing sound?

_____

_____

_____

_____

_____

_____

# Making Sound

## Teacher Notes

### Purpose

The purpose of this assessment probe is to elicit students' ideas about sound production. The task specifically probes to determine whether students recognize that sounds result from vibrations produced by an object or by objects or materials in contact with the object listed.

### Related Concepts

sound, vibration

### Explanation

Sound is a form of energy caused by back-and-forth vibrations. All the objects on the list involve the production of sound as a result of vibration of the object itself or the material it comes in contact with, such as air. Some vibrations are obvious, such as watching the strings

plucked on a guitar. Other vibrations are so small that you can't see them. Some vibrations that cannot be seen can be felt. For example, when you put your fingers over your vocal cords, you can feel the vibrations created when you speak. The loudness of a sound depends on the size of vibrations. The size of vibrations is called their amplitude. Increasing or decreasing the amplitude changes the loudness of a sound. Leaves rustling in a gentle wind create sound with a low amplitude of vibrations, whereas a blaring radio speaker creates sound with a high amplitude. Vibrations also affect the pitch of a sound. Pitch describes how high or low the notes are that are produced by the vibrations of the object. Pitch is affected by changing the frequency of the vibrations—how quickly or slowly the object vibrates. The more vibrations

that occur per second, the higher the frequency and the higher the pitch of the sound.

## Curricular and Instructional Considerations

### Elementary Students

By the end of the elementary grades, most students have had opportunities to learn about sound and how sound is made. Early ideas about sound are connected to position and motion of objects. Teaching and learning about sound is primarily observational and includes having students identify different types of sound and their sources, observe vibration of sound-making objects, and relate loudness and pitch to different types of sound production. The emphasis at this developmental stage is on the objects, even though in some cases it is the air that is in contact with the object that is the source of vibration. Because the notion of vibrating air is a more abstract idea at the elementary level and not directly observable, the national standards focus on vibrating objects at the elementary level. Ideas about vibration and pitch are grade-level expectations described in the national standards. Students at this level often learn about sound through the context of musical instruments. As a result students may become context-bound in their understanding of how sound is produced and may fail to generalize across different examples.

### Middle School Students

In middle school, students build on their elementary grade observations to develop expla-

nations about sound and how it travels. Students at this level begin to understand the abstract notion of air as a source of vibration resulting from contact with an object. Students begin to develop ideas about waves and transmission through different types of materials. The probe is useful at this level to determine whether through prior instruction students developed generalizations about sounds resulting from vibrations or if the context they learned ideas in limited their understanding about sound production.

Topic: What Is Sound?
Go to: www.scilinks.org
Code: USIS45

### High School Students

In high school, students continue to build more sophisticated understandings about sound and sound waves. The probe is useful at this level to determine whether students may still have a limited context in understanding basic ideas about how sound is produced.

### Administering the Probe

Make sure students are familiar with the items on the list. You may wish to remove items that elementary students have little or no familiarity with. This probe can also be used as a card sort. In small groups, students can sort cards listing each item into two groups—those that make sound by vibration and those that do not. Listening carefully to students' discussions with each other as they sort can lend insight into their thinking.

## Related Ideas in *National Science Education Standards* (NRC 1996)

### K–4 Position and Motion of Objects

★ Sound is produced by vibrating objects. The pitch of the sound can be varied by changing the rate of vibration.

### 5–8 Transfer of Energy

• Energy is a property of many substances and is associated with heat, light, electricity, mechanical motion, sound, nuclei, and the nature of a chemical. Energy is transferred in many ways.

## Related Ideas in *Benchmarks for Science Literacy* (AAAS 1993)

### K–2 Motion

★ Things that make sound vibrate.

### 3–5 Motion

• How fast things move differs greatly.

### 6–8 Motion

• Vibrations in materials set up wavelike disturbances that spread away from the source. Sound and earthquake waves are examples. These and other waves move at different speeds in different materials.

## Related Research

• Children's explanations of how sound is produced can be sorted into three groups

that involve (1) physical properties of sound-producing materials, such as thickness, hardness, and elasticity, (2) the size of the force needed to produce the sound, and (3) vibrations (Driver et al. 1994).

• Reference to movement or vibration increases with age (Driver et al. 1994).

• A study by Asoko, Leach, and Scott (1991) used different contexts to have students explain how sound is produced. They used examples such as a guitar string, a horn, cymbals, and two stones clashed together. The results of their study suggest that students do not have a generalized theory of sound being produced by vibration that can be transferred across different contexts. The researchers suggest that "teachers should plan to give children experience of sound production in less obvious contexts as well as in contexts where the vibrations are more clear. It may be useful to allow the children to experiment with applying vibration ideas developed in obvious contexts to less obvious contexts with a view to developing a generalized theory."

• Failure to recognize the role of vibration in sound may be linked to the failure to recognize the involvement of air as a medium in which vibrations are transferred. The role of the ear does not appear to be problematic and may serve as a useful context to develop the idea of vibrations in air (Driver et al. 1994).

## Suggestions for Instruction and Assessment

• Explicitly develop the generalization that

---

★ Indicates a strong match between the ideas elicited by the probe and a national standard's learning goal.

all objects and materials that produce sound vibrate or cause surrounding objects or materials to vibrate, regardless of the examples used to investigate sound production. Be aware that a specific context may limit students' thinking.

- Provide opportunities to experience vibrations in objects where the vibration is not obvious. For example, putting your hand on a hard surface and feeling the vibration as someone pounds on the hard surface is one way of confirming that rigid objects vibrate.

- Connect the idea about how we hear sound to vibrations from the source to the medium that carries the vibrations to our ears.

- Have students investigate objects like tuning forks to observe differences in the vibrations.

## Related NSTA Science Store Publications and NSTA Journal Articles

American Association for the Advancement of Science (AAAS). 2001. *Atlas of science literacy.* (See "Waves," pp. 64–65.) New York: Oxford University Press.

Driver, R., A. Squires, P. Rushworth, and V. Wood-Robinson. 1994. *Making sense of secondary science: Research into children's ideas.* London and New York: RoutledgeFalmer.

Galus, P. 2004. Sensations of sound. *Science Scope* (Nov./Dec.): 44–47.

Levine, S. and L. Johnstone. 2002. *Science experiments with sound and music.* New York: Sterling.

Keeley, P. 2005. *Science curriculum topic study: Bridging the gap between standards and practice.* Thousand Oaks, CA: Corwin Press.

Palmer, D. 2003. Modeling the transmission of sound. *Science Scope* (Apr.): 32.

Robertson, W. 2003. *Sound: Stop faking it! Finally understanding science so you can teach it.* Arlington, VA: NSTA Press.

Stepans, J. 2003. *Targeting students' science misconceptions: Physical science concepts using the conceptual change model.* (See section on sound.) Tampa, FL: Showboard.

### Related Curriculum Topic Study Guide
(Keeley 2005)
"Sound"

## References

American Association for the Advancement of Science (AAAS). 1993. *Benchmarks for science literacy.* New York: Oxford University Press.

Asoko, H. M., J. Leach, and P. H. Scott. 1991. A study of students' understanding of sound 5–16 as an example of action research. Paper prepared for the symposium "Developing Students' Understanding of Science" at the annual conference of the British Educational Research Association, Sept. 2, 1990, London, England.

Driver, R., A. Squires, P. Rushworth, and V. Wood-Robinson. 1994. *Making sense of secondary science: Research into children's ideas.* London and New York: RoutledgeFalmer.

Keeley, P. 2005. *Science curriculum topic study: Bridging the gap between standards and practice.* Thousand Oaks, CA: Corwin Press.

National Research Council (NRC). 1996. *National science education standards.* Washington, DC: National Academy Press.

# Ice Cubes in a Bag

You are having an argument with your friend about what happens to the mass when matter changes from one form to another. To prove your idea, you put three ice cubes in a sealed bag and record the mass of the ice in the bag. You let the ice cubes melt completely. Ten minutes later you record the mass of the water in the bag. Which of the following best describes the result? Circle your prediction.

**A** The mass of the water in the bag will be less than the mass of the ice in the bag.

**B** The mass of the water in the bag will be more than the mass of the ice in the bag.

**C** The mass of the water in the bag will be the same as the mass of the ice cubes in the bag.

Describe your thinking. Provide an explanation for your answer.

_____

_____

_____

_____

_____

_____

_____

_____

_____

_____

_____

# Ice Cubes in a Bag

## Teacher Notes

## Purpose

The purpose of this assessment probe is to elicit students' ideas about conservation of matter in the context of substances and change in state. The probe is designed to find out whether students believe there will be a change in mass when ice changes to liquid water and what their reasoning is to support their prediction. It can also be used to determine whether students connect the idea of a closed system or particle ideas to conservation of mass.

## Related Concepts

conservation of matter, mass, volume, change in state, closed system, atoms, molecules

## Explanation

The best response is C—the mass would be the same. Mass is a measure of the amount of matter in a substance. When water changes from one state to another, the number of molecules of water does not change; therefore, the amount of matter or mass does not change. This rule applies to changes between liquids and gases as well as solids and liquids. A change in state is a change in the average motion and arrangement of the molecules, not the number of molecules or their mass. Also, the sealed bag implies a closed system (even though plastic bags are semipermeable). If a system is closed, then no new matter can get into the bag and nothing can get out. Therefore, the total mass remains the same since nothing is added or subtracted. Conservation of matter is a physical principle, applied to ordinary physical and chemical changes, that states that matter can-

**5**

not be created or destroyed. This principle is used to explain a variety of chemical, biological, and geologic changes.

## Curricular and Instructional Considerations

### Elementary Students

Conservation of matter ideas begin in the elementary grades with investigations of objects or familiar materials. Knowing that the sum of the parts weighs the same as the whole is a grade-level expectation in the national standards. While students are not ready at this level to use particle ideas or terms such as *mass*, they may use parts and wholes reasoning—for example, the water "parts" came from the ice, so nothing new was added. Students at this age are familiar with the idea that ice can change to water and vice versa. Mass is a concept that is usually not developed until middle school. If this probe is used with elementary students, consider using the familiar term *weight*.

### Middle School Students

In middle school, students progress from ideas about conservation of matter using objects and materials to substances, like water. They begin to use particle ideas and closed systems to support their explanations. They develop the concept of mass linked to a conception of matter. They use their ideas to explain conservation of matter with physical or chemical changes in substances as the context. Knowing that matter is conserved during ordinary chemical and physical interactions is a grade-level ex-

pectation in the national standards. This probe is useful for determining what types of misconceptions students have about matter during a change in state.

Topic: **Changes in State**
Go to: *www.scilinks.org*
Code: **USIS51**

### High School Students

Grade-level expectations for achieving conservation of matter ideas culminate in middle school. By high school, students are expected to know that matter is conserved in ordinary interactions and changes. Since conservation of matter explains several phenomena encountered in high school, this probe is useful in finding out if students have a basic conception of matter conservation so it can be used to explain biological, chemical, and geologic phenomena. Chemistry students may be able to recite the law of conservation of matter and use conservation reasoning to balance chemical equations; yet, when confronted with an ordinary change like ice melting, they may revert back to their misconceptions.

### Administering the Probe

This probe is one of several conservation of matter probes set in different contexts and at various levels of sophistication. At any grade level you might consider using props with this probe. Show students the ice cubes in a ziplock plastic bag before and after they have melted or use before-and-after digital photographs. Use the term *weight* instead of *mass* if younger students are not familiar with the latter term. You might encourage older students to use particle ideas in their explanations. This probe can be combined with or follow a less sophisticated context such as the probe "Cookie Crumbles" (p. 61). It can also be used in comparison to a different physical change such as dissolving in "Lemonade" (p. 55) or a change to a biological context such as "Seedlings in a Jar" (p. 67).

## Related Ideas in *National Science Education Standards* (NRC 1996)

### K–4 Properties of Objects and Materials

- Objects have many observable properties, including size, weight, and shape. Those properties can be measured using tools, such as rulers, balances, and thermometers.
- Materials can exist in different states—solid, liquid, and gas.

### 5–8 Properties and Changes in Properties of Matter

- In chemical reactions, the total mass is conserved.

### 9–12 Structure and Properties of Matter

- Matter is made up of minute particles called atoms.

## Related Ideas in *Benchmarks for Science Literacy* (AAAS 1993)

### K–2 The Earth

★ Water can be a liquid or a solid and can go back and forth from one form to another. If water is turned into ice and then the ice is allowed to melt, the amount of water is the same as it was before freezing.

### 3–5 Structure of Matter

- No matter how parts of an object are assembled, the weight of the whole object made is always the same as the sum of the parts, and when a thing is broken into parts, the parts have the same total weight as the original thing.

### 3–5 Constancy and Change

- Some features of things may stay the same even when other features change.

### 6–8 Structure of Matter

★ No matter how substances within a closed system interact with one another, or how they combine or break apart, the total weight of the system remains the same. The idea of atoms explains the conservation of matter. If the number of atoms stays the same no matter how they are rearranged, then their total mass stays the same.

## Related Research

- Student understanding of conservation of matter begins with qualitative notions. In a study conducted by Stavy (1990), by fifth grade, students qualitatively understood matter was conserved when it changed

---

★ Indicates a strong match between the ideas elicited by the probe and a national standard's learning goal.

from a solid to a liquid but they were just beginning to understand the change quantitatively (AAAS 1993).

- Children will have difficulty with conservation of matter if they cannot distinguish between weight and density (AAAS 1993).

- A study by Holding (1987) investigated students' conceptions of mass. Some students confuse the word *mass* with the word *massive* and hence their conception of change in mass was dominated by the bulk appearance of the material.

- A study by Osborne and Cosgrove (1983) found that some children regard the liquid form of a material as differing in weight from the same amount of mass as its solid form.

- This probe is based on a study similar to one conducted by Stavy (1987). Students were shown two samples of ice that had the same weight. One sample was melted and then students were asked to compare the melted sample with the unmelted ice. The percentage of students who used conservation reasoning increased with age: 5% ages 5 and 6, 50% age 7, and 75% age 10 (Driver et al. 1994).

- Stavy and Tirosh (1995) identified intuitive rules students use to reason conservation problems. If students think of the water as being more spread out, they may use the rule "more A equals more B" to account for increased mass since it appears the water is more spread out or taking up more space than the ice.

## Suggestions for Instruction and Assessment

- This probe can be followed up with an inquiry-based investigation. Ask the question, encourage students to commit to a prediction, and then test it. The dissonance involved in discovering that the mass remains the same should be followed with opportunities for students to discuss their ideas and resolve the dissonance.

- In elementary grades the study of changes in state between liquids and solids should be combined with developing the idea that the weight of the changed matter remains the same. Nothing new is added and nothing is taken away.

- Help students recognize other logical rules to explain mass conservation, such as the idea of a closed system: If nothing can get in or out, then the mass of the system must remain the same regardless of the change. Compare and contrast the change in an open versus a closed system where some of the water is allowed to evaporate over time.

- When students are ready, later in middle school, teach the idea of atoms along with ideas such as conservation of matter.

- Modify the probe to present students with the opposite change—an amount of liquid in a bag that is placed in a freezer to form a solid.

- Elicit students' ideas about multiple back-and-forth changes in state—melting, then freezing, repeated two or three times. Will their ideas change if there are multiple transitions between states?

## Related NSTA Science Store Publications and NSTA Journal Articles

American Association for the Advancement of Science (AAAS). 2001. *Atlas of science literacy.* (See "Conservation of Matter," pp. 56–57.) New York: Oxford University Press

Driver, R., Squires, A., Rushworth, P., and Wood-Robinson, V. 1994. *Making sense of secondary science: Research into children's ideas.* London and New York: RoutledgeFalmer.

Keeley, P., F. Eberle, and L. Farrin. 2005. Formative assessment probes: Uncovering students' ideas in science. *Science Scope* (Jan.): 18–21.

Stavy, R., and D. Tirosh. 1995. *How students (mis-) understand science and mathematics: Intuitive rules.* New York: Teachers College Press.

### Related Curriculum Topic Study Guides
(Keeley 2005)
"Conservation of Matter"
"States of Matter"
"Physical Properties and Change"

## References

American Association for the Advancement of Science (AAAS). 1993. *Benchmarks for science literacy.* New York: Oxford University Press.

Driver, R., A. Squires, P. Rushworth, and V. Wood-Robinson. 1994. *Making sense of secondary science: Research into children's ideas.* London and New York: RoutledgeFalmer.

Holding, B. 1987. Investigation of school children's understanding of the process of dissolving with special reference to the conservation of mass and the development of atomistic ideas. Ph.D. diss., University of Leeds, UK.

Keeley, P. 2005. *Science curriculum topic study: Bridging the gap between standards and practice.* Thousand Oaks, CA: Corwin Press.

National Research Council (NRC). (1996). *National science education standards.* Washington, DC: National Academy Press.

Osborne R., and M. Cosgrove. 1983. Children's conceptions of the changes of state of water. *Journal of Research in Science Teaching* 20 (9): 825–838.

Stavy, R. 1987. Acquisition of conservation of matter. Paper presented at the Second Conference on Misconceptions, Cornell University.

Stavy, R. 1990. Children's conceptions of changes in the state of matter: From liquid (or solid) to gas. *Journal of Research in Science Teaching* 27: 247–266.

Stavy, R., and D. Tirosh. 1995. *How students (mis-) understand science and mathematics: Intuitive rules.* New York: Teachers College Press.

# Lemonade

A glass of unsweetened lemonade weighs 255 grams. A spoonful of sugar is weighed before stirring it into the lemonade. The sugar weighs 25 grams. Predict how much you think the sweetened lemonade will weigh after you stir in the sugar.

Please circle the best answer.

**A** It will weigh slightly less than 255 grams but more than 230 grams.

**B** It will weigh slightly more than 255 grams but less than 280 grams.

**C** It will weigh 230 grams.

**D** It will weigh 280 grams.

**E** It will weigh the same: 255 grams.

Describe your thinking. Provide an explanation for your answer.

_____

_____

_____

_____

_____

_____

_____

_____

_____

_____

# Lemonade

## Teacher Notes

## Purpose

The purpose of this assessment probe is to elicit students' ideas about conservation of matter in the context of dissolving. The probe is designed to find out what students think about the total weight or mass of a solution when a solute, such as sugar, seemingly "disappears" in a solvent.

## Related Concepts

conservation of matter, physical change, mass, weight, dissolving

## Explanation

The best response is D. The sweetened lemonade contains the 25 grams of sugar, added to the 255 grams of unsweetened lemonade. Even though you cannot see the sugar because it is dissolved, it is there. The visible sugar substance breaks down into sugar molecules, which cannot be seen, that are attracted to the water molecules. A basic application of the principle of the conservation of matter explains what happened to the total weight or mass—the sum of the parts, in this case the unsweetened lemonade and the sugar, is equal to the whole (the sweetened lemonade).

## Curricular and Instructional Considerations

### Elementary Students

Weight conservation ideas are developed in the elementary grades using objects or familiar substances. Mixing sugar in water or observing other water-based solutions is a common experience for elementary students. They see the sugar "disappear" but may not understand where it goes. "Parts and wholes" ideas are used to help students develop beginning ideas about conservation of matter. This probe is useful in eliciting early ideas about what happens to substances that dissolve.

## Middle School Students

In middle school, students develop the concept of mass and use the idea of conservation of matter in the context of familiar physical or chemical changes with substances. Mixtures and solutions are commonly investigated by students at this grade level. While the National Science Education Standards (NRC 1996) explicitly mention conservation of matter in the context of chemical reactions, it is still important to find out if students understand that mass is conserved in ordinary physical changes. At this level they may begin to use the idea of molecules or simple particulate models to explain what happens when the sugar dissolves, although nature of attraction between sugar and water molecules is too complex at this level. The probe is useful in determining if misconceptions still exist even after elementary grades instruction.

## High School Students

Students at this grade level develop a more sophisticated picture of a particulate model of matter and dissolving. They begin to develop an understanding of hydrogen bonds and the attraction between molecules of a solute and

solvent. Their conservation reasoning about solutions becomes more sophisticated as they combine their understanding of a particulate model of matter with conservation of dissolved substances. This probe is useful in determining if students at this level use their sophisticated ideas to reason through the problem situation or if they revert back to their prior conceptions.

**Topic: Changes in Matter**
**Go to: www.scilinks.org**
**Code: USIS57**

## Administering the Probe

Be sure students understand that the sugar and the unsweetened lemonade are weighed individually before the sugar is added to the lemonade. You may demonstrate what happens when you mix sugar with water so that students see that the sugar is no longer visible. Listen for students who accept the idea that the sugar exists in the sweetened lemonade but may believe it no longer has weight. In other words, they may believe that matter is conserved but weight is not. The word *mass* may be substituted for *weight* at the middle level and above.

## Related Ideas in *National Science Education Standards* (NRC 1996)

. . . . . . . . . . . . . . . . . . . . . . . . . . . . . .

### K–4 Properties of Objects and Materials

- Objects have many observable properties, including size, weight, shape, color, temperature, and the ability to react with other

substances. Those properties can be measured using tools such as rulers, balances, and thermometers.

- Objects are made of one or more materials.

### 5–8 Properties and Changes in Properties of Matter

- A substance has characteristic properties such as solubility.

## Related Ideas in *Benchmarks for Science Literacy* (AAAS 1993)

· · · · · · · · · · · · · · · · · · · · · · · · · · · ·

### 3–5 Structure of Matter

★ No matter how parts of an object are assembled, the weight of the whole object made is always the same as the sum of the parts, and when a thing is broken into parts, the parts have the same total weight as the original thing.

★ Materials may be composed of parts that are too small to be seen without magnification.

### 6–8 Structure of Matter

★ No matter how substances within a closed system interact with one another, or how they combine or break apart, the total weight of the system remains the same. The idea of atoms explains the conservation of matter. If the number of atoms stays the same no matter how they are rearranged, then their total mass stays the same.

### 9–12 Structure of Matter

- An enormous variety of biological, chemical, and physical phenomena can be ex-

plained by changes in the arrangement and motion of atoms and molecules.

## Related Research

- Students' ideas may be affected by their conception of dissolving and solutions. Some students believe that sugar just mixes with water to become the same substance (Driver et al. 1994).

- Several researchers have investigated students' conservation ideas in the context of dissolving. Discrepancies have been found between students who conserve a substance but fail to conserve weight. Holding (1987) found a high percentage of eight-year-olds believed that a solute was somehow present in some form when it was dissolved. When he probed students about the weight of the solution, however, only 50% of those who thought the sugar was still there felt it had weight. One reason for this appears to be that students thought the dissolved sugar was in a "suspended" state; thus it was not pressing down on the container as "weight" (Driver et al. 1994).

- Driver (1985) described three different types of reasoning students use in this type of problem: (1) sugar disappears into "nothing" when dissolved, (2) mass and volume are confused, and (3) sugar is still present in the solution but is lighter.

## Suggestions for Instruction and Assessment

- This probe can be followed up as an inquiry-based investigation. Ask the ques-

---

★ Indicates a strong match between the ideas elicited by the probe and a national standard's learning goal.

tion, encourage students to commit to a prediction, and then test it. The dissonance involved in discovering that the weight or mass remains the same should be followed with opportunities for students to discuss their ideas and resolve the dissonance.

- With older students, link the idea of matter to mass. Help students understand that conservation of matter and conservation of mass are the same principle. If they accept the idea that the sugar is present in the solution, then because the matter is present it must have the same mass as it did before it was dissolved.

- Ask students to draw "particulate pictures" to show and explain what happens to the sugar and where it goes when it dissolves in water.

- If student experiences involve only colorless solutions, such as salt or sugar in water, it may reinforce the notion that the substance "disappears." Provide colored solutes such as coffee or drink crystals and use the presence of color to help students understand that this is additional evidence for the matter existing, even though its form has changed. However, accepting the evidence that the matter is there does not always mean students will accept the idea that the total mass or weight does not change.

## Related NSTA Science Store Publications and NSTA Journal Articles

American Association for the Advancement of Science (AAAS). 2001. *Atlas of science literacy.* (See "Conservation of Matter," pp. 54–55.) New

York: Oxford University Press.

American Chemical Society. 2005. *Inquiry in action: Investigating matter through inquiry.* 2nd ed. Washington, DC: American Chemical Society.

Driver, R., A. Squires, P. Rushworth, and V. Wood-Robinson. 1994. *Making sense of secondary science: Research into children's ideas.* London and New York: RoutledgeFalmer.

Keeley, P. 2005. *Science curriculum topic study: Bridging the gap between standards and practice.* Thousand Oaks, CA: Corwin Press.

Keeley, P., F. Eberle, and L. Farrin. 2005. Formative assessment probes: Uncovering students' ideas in science. *Science Scope* (Jan.): 18–21.

**Related Curriculum Topic Study Guides**

(Keeley 2005)
"Conservation of Matter"
"Mixtures and Solutions"
"Physical Properties and Change"

## References

American Association for the Advancement of Science (AAAS). 1993. *Benchmarks for science literacy.* New York: Oxford University Press.

Driver, R. 1985. Beyond appearances: The conservation of matter. In *Children's ideas in science,* eds. R. Driver, E. Guesne, and A. Tiberghien. Milton Keynes, UK: Open University Press.

Driver, R., A. Squires, P. Rushworth, and V. Wood-Robinson. 1994. *Making sense of secondary science: Research into children's ideas.* London and New York: RoutledgeFalmer.

Holding, B. 1987. Investigation of school children's

understanding of the process of dissolving with special reference to the conservation of mass and the development of atomistic ideas. Ph.D. diss., University of Leeds, UK.

Keeley, P. 2005. *Science curriculum topic study: Bridging the gap between standards and practice.* Thousand Oaks, CA: Corwin Press.

National Research Council (NRC). 1996. *National science education standards.* Washington DC: National Academy Press.

# Cookie Crumbles

Imagine you have a whole cookie. You break the cookie into tiny pieces and crumbs. You weigh all of the pieces and crumbs. How do you think the weight of the whole cookie compares to the total weight of all the cookie crumbs? Circle the best answer.

**A** The whole cookie weighs more than all of the cookie crumbs.

**B** All of the cookie crumbs weigh more than the whole cookie.

**C** The whole cookie and all of the cookie crumbs weigh the same.

Describe your thinking. Provide an explanation for your answer.

_____

_____

_____

_____

_____

_____

_____

_____

_____

_____

# Cookie Crumbles

## Teacher Notes

## Purpose

The purpose of this assessment probe is to find out students' ideas about conservation of matter using ordinary objects such as a cookie. The probe is specifically designed to find out whether students believe there will be a change in weight when a whole object is broken up into many small pieces.

## Related Concepts

conservation of matter, weight, physical change

## Explanation

The best response is C—the weight would be the same. The total weight of the parts, in this case the cookie crumbs, is equal to the weight of the unbroken cookie. The only thing that changed was the shape or arrangement of the

cookie; no new matter was added or taken away. Conservation of matter is a physical principle that applies to ordinary changes in objects as well as to physical and chemical changes in substances. In both cases, matter cannot be created or destroyed in an ordinary physical or chemical change.

## Curricular and Instructional Considerations

### Elementary Students

Conservation ideas about changes in objects or materials are developed in the upper elementary grades. Knowing that the sum of the parts

of an object is the same as the whole object is a grade-level expectation in the national standards. The term *weight*, instead of *mass*, is used here as students below grade 5 may not be familiar with the term *mass*. Using the word *mass* before students are ready to comprehend its meaning may cause students to confuse the word with *massive*, thus equating mass with size. This probe is useful in determining students' preconceptions about conservation of parts and wholes before formal instruction.

### Middle School Students

At this level, students progress from conservation of matter ideas about objects to conservation of matter ideas involving changes in substances. Although this probe targets an elementary level of sophistication, it can be used with middle school students to see if they are ready to use conservation reasoning to explain changes in substances, by first accepting the idea of conservation of matter with ordinary objects.

### High School Students

This probe is designed for lower grades. However, if high school students have difficulty with the other conservation of matter probes ("Ice Cubes in a Bag," "Lemonade," and "Seedings in a Jar"), teachers may consider going all the way back to eliciting their ideas about conservation of matter with this less sophisticated probe. Student work from this task is useful in having K–12 grade-level conversations about conservation-related ideas and how they develop over time. Although the sophistication of the

context changes, teachers can see the progression of development in students' thinking by comparing "Cookie Crumbles" with "Ice Cubes in a Bag" (p. 49).

**SCI LINKS.**
THE WORLD'S A CLICK AWAY
**Topic: Conservation of Matter**
**Go to:** *www.scilinks.org*
**Code: USIS63**

### Administering the Probe

The conservation of matter probes are set in different contexts and at various levels of sophistication. Teachers may want to combine reasoning about objects, such as in this task, with reasoning about substances such as in "Ice Cubes in a Bag" (p. 49). For younger students it may be helpful to use props with this probe. Show students a whole cookie and then break the cookie into crumbs so that they have a visual context. Make sure students know that all of the crumbs are weighed.

## Related Ideas in *National Science Education Standards* (NRC 1996)

. . . . . . . . . . . . . . . . . . . . . . . . . . . . . . .

### K–4 Properties of Objects and Materials

* Objects have many observable properties, including size, weight, and shape. Those properties can be measured using tools such as rulers, balances, and thermometers.

## Related Ideas in *Benchmarks for Science Literacy* (AAAS 1993)

. . . . . . . . . . . . . . . . . . . . . . . . . . . . . . .

### 3–5 Structure of Matter

★ No matter how parts of an object are as-

---

★ Indicates a strong match between the ideas elicited by the probe and a national standard's learning goal.

sembled, the weight of the whole object made is always the same as the sum of the parts, and when a thing is broken into parts, the parts have the same total weight as the original thing.

### 3–5 Constancy and Change

- Some features of things may stay the same even when other features change.

## Related Research

- Several studies have shown that the way a physical change is perceived may influence whether students regard material as being conserved during the change (Driver et al. 1994).

- Although the cookie is broken into crumbs, not powdered, students' ideas about powdered forms of objects may be related to students' ideas in this task. It has been found that children view the change of a bulk solid to a powdered solid as likely to result in a decrease in mass (Driver et al. 1994).

- Stavy and Tirosh (1995) investigated intuitive rules used by students of all ages to explain conservation problems. Because the broken cookie looks like there is less material present than the intact cookie, they may reason that the weight would be less.

## Suggestions for Instruction and Assessment

- This probe can be followed up with as an inquiry investigation after asking students to commit to a prediction. Students can

test their ideas with a cookie.

- Provide elementary students with a variety of opportunities to weigh whole objects and then take them apart, weigh their pieces, and compare the weights.

- In addition to comparing weights, have students compare numbers of parts that make up an object. For example, have students put together Legos, blocks, or Unifix Cubes in one shape, count the number of pieces, take it apart and rebuild it differently. Ask them if any pieces (a precursor analogy to matter) were lost or gained. Have them prove their ideas by counting the number of pieces before and after. This helps students develop an early conception that the same amount of "matter" is there, a precursor idea to developing a concept of mass based on particles.

## Related NSTA Science Store Publications and NSTA Journal Articles

American Association for the Advancement of Science (AAAS). 2001. *Atlas of science literacy.* (See "Conservation of Matter," pp. 56–57). New York: Oxford University Press.

Keeley, P. 2005. *Science curriculum topic study: Bridging the gap between standards and practice.* Thousand Oaks, CA: Corwin Press.

Keeley, P., F. Eberle, and L. Farrin. 2005. Formative assessment probes: Uncovering students' ideas in science. *Science Scope* (Jan.): 18–21.

Stavy, R., and D. Tirosh. 1995. *How students (mis-) understand science and mathematics: Intuitive rules.* New York: Teachers College Press.

---

★ Indicates a strong match between the ideas elicited by the probe and a national standard's learning goal.

Related Curriculum Topic Study Guides
(Keeley 2005)
"Conservation of Matter"
"Physical Properties and Change"

## References

American Association for the Advancement of Science (AAAS). 1993. *Benchmarks for science literacy.* New York: Oxford University Press.

Driver, R., A. Squires, P. Rushworth, and V. Wood-Robinson. 1994. *Making sense of secondary science: Research into children's ideas.* London and New York: RoutledgeFalmer.

Keeley, P. 2005. *Science curriculum topic study: Bridging the gap between standards and practice.* Thousand Oaks, CA: Corwin Press.

National Research Council (NRC). 1996. *National science education standards.* Washington, DC: National Academy Press.

Stavy, R., and D. Tirosh. 1995. *How students (mis-) understand science and mathematics: Intuitive rules.* New York: Teachers College Press.

# Seedlings in a Jar

Imagine you have a sealed jar containing five bean seeds, air, and a moist paper towel. Nothing can get in or out of the jar. The total mass of the jar and its contents is 500 grams.

Imagine the same jar with its contents 12 days later. During that time the jar remained sealed. Nothing could get in or out of the jar. The seeds have germinated to form 6-centimeter seedlings. The total mass of the jar and its contents after the 12 days is recorded.

Circle the statement that is the best comparison of the total mass of the jar and its contents before and after the seeds sprouted to form seedlings:

**A** The total mass of the original jar with seeds will be more than the total mass of the jar with the seedlings.

**B** The total mass of the original jar with seeds will be less than the total mass of the jar with the seedlings.

**C** There will be no change in the total mass of the jar with seedlings after 12 days.

Describe your thinking. Provide an explanation for your answer.

_____

_____

_____

_____

_____

# Seedlings in a Jar

## Teacher Notes

## Purpose

The purpose of this assessment probe is to elicit students' ideas about conservation of matter in a closed system. The probe is designed to find out if students can transfer ideas about conservation of matter in a closed system to a life science context. Even though transformation of matter ideas related to food, growth, photosynthesis, and respiration are embedded within the task, students do not need to use this knowledge if they grasp the fundamental idea that no new atoms are added or taken away within the closed system.

## Related Concepts

conservation of matter, mass, atoms or molecules, chemical change, closed system

## Explanation

The best response is C. The probe explicitly states that nothing can get in or out of the jar—it is a closed system. An interaction occurs as food contained in the seed is transformed chemically into new matter that makes up the plant structures of the seedling. An interaction also occurs between water, oxygen, and carbon dioxide in a cycle of photosynthesis and respiration that results in the building of additional plant material. All of this occurs inside a closed system. The atoms that made up the original matter in the seed, air, and water are rearranged and found in new plant structures, but no mass is added or lost in the total system.

## Curricular and Instructional Considerations

### Elementary Students

Conservation of matter in the elementary grades focuses on parts and wholes of objects and change of state during freezing and melting. While the context for this probe is rather sophisticated for elementary students, it can be used to find out elementary students' intuitive ideas about the change from seed to seedling in a closed system.

### Middle School Students

According to the national standards, by the end of middle school all students should know that matter or mass is conserved in a closed system as well as in chemical reactions (including biological chemical reactions). Conservation ideas about objects begin in elementary grades and increase in cognitive sophistication as the ideas of atoms, interactions, transformations, and closed systems are considered. Transformation of matter is addressed in middle school, although it remains a difficult concept and one in which students may have difficulty applying conservation reasoning. Students are apt to use intuitive reasoning of more A (more size) means more B (more mass) for this probe since there is a very dramatic visual difference between the size of the seeds versus the size of the seedlings. The notion that gases are involved in the transformation may be missing.

### High School Students

Conservation of matter at the high school level

is implicit in other matter-related ideas in biological, physical, and geological contexts. The probe is useful in determining whether students can transfer conservation of matter ideas in contexts other than physical science, where they are most apt to encounter the concept through prior instruction. It is also useful in determining whether students recognize a closed system as justification for matter being conserved. Students do not have to use complex ideas about respiration, photosynthesis, and transformation of matter if they recognize that matter cannot enter or leave a closed system.

Topic: Chemical Changes
Go to: *www.scilinks.org*
Code: USIS69

### Administering the Probe

Make sure students understand that the jar is sealed and nothing can enter or escape from the jar. It may help to have visual props for this probe. Seal five bean seeds in a jar containing a wet paper towel. Put in a dark place for a few days and allow the seeds to sprout. After the first leaves emerge, place in sunlight for several days until the seedlings fill the jar. Have students observe the seeds before and after and consider what happens to the mass.

## Related Ideas in *National Science Education Standards* (NRC 1996)

### K–4 Properties of Objects and Materials

- Objects have many observable properties, including size, weight, and shape.

Those properties can be measured using tools such as rulers, balances, and thermometers.

## 5–8 Properties and Changes in Properties of Matter

★ In chemical reactions, the total mass is conserved.

## 9–12 Structure and Properties of Matter

• Matter is made up of minute particles called atoms.

## Related Ideas in *Benchmarks for Science Literacy* (AAAS 1993)

. . . . . . . . . . . . . . . . . . . . . . . . . . . . . . .

### 3–5 Structure of Matter

• No matter how parts of an object are assembled, the weight of the whole object made is always the same as the sum of the parts, and when a thing is broken into parts, the parts have the same total weight as the original thing.

### 6–8 Structure of Matter

★ No matter how substances within a closed system interact with one another, or how they combine or break apart, the total weight of the system remains the same. The idea of atoms explains the conservation of matter. If the number of atoms stays the same no matter how they are rearranged, then their total mass stays the same.

### 6–8 Flow of Matter and Energy

• Food provides molecules that serve as fuel and building material for all organisms.

## Related Research

• Studies show that the way students perceive a change may influence their ideas about conservation during that change. For example, if their view is dominated by the appearance of new material, such as the seedling structures, then they may think mass has been added (AAAS 1993).

• Research indicates that few students view conservation of matter in different contexts such as photosynthesis, assimilation of food, and respiration. This may also be related to difficulties students have in attributing growth, such as the seedling growing from the seed, to food being transformed to make up the new material (Driver et al. 1994).

• Stavy and Tirosh (1995) identified an intuitive rule, "more A equals more B," that helps explain why students believe the mass will increase. Since the seedling obviously looks like it has more mass than the mere seeds, students intuitively reason that the mass would be more.

## Suggestions for Instruction and Assessment

• Have students carry out an investigation to test the idea they committed to in the probe and use their findings to resolve the differences between their prediction and results.

---

★ Indicates a strong match between the ideas elicited by the probe and a national standard's learning goal.

- Help students understand that seeds contain food for the seedling and that this food is used for energy and transformed into new structures, until the plants' leaves can make food for the plant. Food making and growth of plants can be tied to conservation of matter so students can see how the ideas apply to a life science context as well. If conservation of matter is taught only in a physical science context, students may fail to make the transfer.

- Develop an understanding of open versus closed systems and explicitly link conservation of matter to changes within a closed system.

- Help students understand the idea that there is air in the jar that is also being transformed. In the early grades, explicitly develop the idea that air is a substance and has mass; revisit this idea throughout the grade levels.

- Help students understand that transformation of food in a biological system is a type of chemical reaction. Tie the idea of conservation in chemical reactions to biological processes such as photosynthesis, respiration, and transformation of sugars into new substances.

## Related NSTA Science Store Publications and NSTA Journal Articles

American Association for the Advancement of Science (AAAS). 2001. *Atlas of science literacy*. (See "Flow of Matter in Ecosystems," pp. 76–77, and "Conservation of Matter," pp. 56–57.)

New York: Oxford University Press.

Driver, R., A. Squires, P. Rushworth, and V. Wood-Robinson. 1994. *Making sense of secondary science: Research into children's ideas*. London and New York: RoutledgeFalmer.

Keeley, P. 2005. *Science curriculum topic study: Bridging the gap between standards and practice*. Thousand Oaks, CA: Corwin Press.

Keeley, P., F. Eberle, and L. Farrin. 2005. Formative assessment probes: Uncovering students' ideas in science. *Science Scope* 28 (4): 18–21.

Stavy, R., and D. Tirosh. 1995. *How students (mis-) understand science and mathematics: Intuitive rules*. New York: Teachers College Press.

### Related Curriculum Topic Study Guides

(Keeley 2005)
"Conservation of Matter"
"Cycling of Matter in Ecosystems"
"Photosynthesis and Respiration"

## References

American Association for the Advancement of Science (AAAS). 1993. *Benchmarks for science literacy*. New York: Oxford University Press.

Driver, R., A. Squires, P. Rushworth, and V. Wood-Robinson. 1994. *Making sense of secondary science: Research into children's ideas*. London and New York: RoutledgeFalmer.

Keeley, P. 2005. *Science curriculum topic study: Bridging the gap between standards and practice*. Thousand Oaks, CA: Corwin Press.

National Research Council (NRC). 1996. *National science education standards*. Washington, DC:

National Academy Press.

Stavy, R., and D. Tirosh. 1995. *How students (mis-) understand science and mathematics: Intuitive rules.* New York: Teachers College Press.

# Is It Melting?

The list below involves situations that cause changes in materials. The materials are *italicized*. Put an X next to the situations in which the *italicized* materials undergo melting.

____ **A** Putting a bowl of frozen *ice cream* in the sun.

____ **B** Sawing *wood* to make sawdust.

____ **C** Dissolving *salt* in water.

____ **D** Adding a *LifeSaver* candy to a glass of warm water.

____ **E** *Water* evaporating from a pan.

____ **F** Dissolving a *sugar cube* in a cup of hot tea.

____ **G** Pouring vinegar on *baking soda*.

____ **H** Sucking on a *lollipop* or other *hard candy*.

____ **I** Holding an *ice cube* in your hand.

Explain your thinking. Describe the "rule" or reasoning you used to decide if something melts.

_____

_____

_____

_____

_____

_____

# Is It Melting?

## Teacher Notes

## Purpose

The purpose of this assessment probe is to elicit students' ideas about the physical process of melting. The probe is designed to find out if students recognize melting as a change in state from solid to liquid that involves one substance or if they confuse it with other physical changes, such as dissolving, that involve two substances.

## Related Concepts

melting, dissolving, change in state, physical change, heat

## Explanation

There are two examples of melting—A and I. Melting is a process in which a solid undergoes changes in the arrangement and average motion of particles to become a liquid. In order to melt, a substance needs to absorb heat energy. This heat energy increases the average motion of the particles, resulting in a change in state. Dissolving is not a change in state. When solid materials dissolve they involve intermolecular forces that help break down substances into smaller particles (such as molecules or ions). Dissolving requires two materials to be mixed

together—a solute and solvent. This differs from melting, which is the result of one material gaining energy.

## Curricular and Instructional Considerations

### Elementary Students

At this level students are exploring a variety of physical changes, including melting and dissolving. The distinction between the two is a sophisticated idea for this level. However, the probe is useful in determining early ideas about various phenomena that appear to "melt" and whether young children confuse the idea of melting with dissolving.

### Middle School Students

At this level students begin to use particulate ideas to explain both change in state and dissolving. The idea of addition of heat energy and the motion of particles is used to explain physical changes such as melting and boiling. However, students at this level may still confuse dissolving with melting, particularly when a liquid is involved in some way. This probe is useful in determining students' ideas prior to developing formal concepts and ideas related to these physical processes.

### High School Students

As students encounter formal concepts and ideas in chemistry dealing with the attraction among and between particles and their arrangements, and develop a more sophisticated particulate model, they may overcome their earlier

ideas about dissolving and melting being the same process. The idea that particles change state (e.g., melting) as they absorb heat and increase their average motion is a grade-level expectation in the national standards. This probe is useful in finding out if students have changed previously held ideas or if they still hold on to their preconceptions, even after formal instruction.

Topic: Changes in State
Go to: *www.scilinks.org*
Code: USIS51

### Administering the Probe

Be sure students are familiar with the phenomena described in the various examples. Eliminate phenomena that are unfamiliar. This probe may be used as a card sort, having students discuss in small groups whether the example is one of melting or something else, while the teacher observes and listens to students' reasoning.

## Related Ideas in *National Science Education Standards* (NRC 1996)

### K–4 Properties of Objects and Materials

- Materials can exist in different states: solid, liquid, and gas. Some common materials, such as water, can be changed from one state to another by heating or cooling.

### 5–8 Properties and Changes of Properties in Matter

- A substance has characteristic properties such as density, boiling point, and solu-

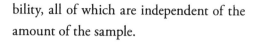

bility, all of which are independent of the amount of the sample.

### 9–12 Structure and Properties of Matter

- Solids, liquids, and gases differ in the distances and angles between molecules or atoms and therefore the energy that binds them together.
- The physical properties of compounds reflect the nature of the interactions among their molecules.

## Related Ideas in *Benchmarks for Science Literacy* (AAAS 1993)

. . . . . . . . . . . . . . . . . . . . . . . . . . . . . .

### 3–5 Structure of Matter

- Heating and cooling cause changes in the properties of materials.

### 6–8 Structure of Matter

- ★ Atoms and molecules are perpetually in motion. In liquids, the atoms or molecules have higher energy, are more loosely connected, and can slide past one another.

### 9–12 Structure of Matter

- An enormous variety of biological, chemical, and physical phenomena can be explained by changes in the arrangement and motion of atoms and molecules.
- The configuration of atoms in a molecule determines the molecule's properties. Shapes are particularly important in how large molecules interact with others.

## Related Research

- Young children have difficulty distinguishing between melting and dissolving. "Although two materials are required for the dissolving process, children tend to focus only on the solid and they regard the process as melting" (Driver et al. 1994, p. 80). When things dissolve they frequently describe them as "melting away."
- When children are probed after using the term *melts,* many describe it as being similar to ice "going runny" (Driver et al. 1994).
- Cosgrove and Osborne (1980) sampled 8- to 17-year-old children and found that they regarded melting and dissolving as similar processes since they were both gradual. They also found that melting was unconnected to the concept of a particular melting point.

## Suggestions for Instruction and Assessment

- When teaching about physical changes, have students come up with a "rule" that can be used to identify a type of physical change. For example, help students recognize that dissolving involves two materials whereas a phase change involves one. This can explicitly be used to help students develop a rule to decide if something dissolves or melts.
- Have students come up with familiar phrases that use words like *melt.* For example, "melts in your mouth" might be scientifically true of ice but not of hard candy.

---

★ Indicates a strong match between the ideas elicited by the probe and a national standard's learning goal.

- Help students understand that not only materials that initially appear "cold" melt. For example, butter at room temperature may begin to melt.

- Connect the idea of melting to absorbing heat energy. However, be sure students do not confuse heating a liquid in order to dissolve a solid with melting.

- Ask older students to draw a "particle picture" that shows what is happening to the particles in each of the examples. Look for evidence of ideas about the motion of the particles versus the substance breaking down into individual particles.

- Pay careful attention to the words students use in activities that involve melting or dissolving. The way in which a student uses a word like *melting* is indicative of the meaning it holds for him or her.

## Related NSTA Science Store Publications and NSTA Journal Articles

Driver, R., A. Squires, P. Rushworth, and V. Wood-Robinson. 1994. *Making sense of secondary science: Research into children's ideas.* London and New York: RoutledgeFalmer.

Keeley, P. 2005. *Science curriculum topic study: Bridging the gap between standards and practice.* Thousand Oaks, CA: Corwin Press.

Ontario Science Centre. 1995. *Solids, liquids, and gases.* Tonawanda, NY: Kids Can Press.

### Related Curriculum Topic Study Guides
(Keeley 2005)
"States of Matter"
"Mixtures and Solutions"
"Physical Properties and Change"
"Liquids"

## References

American Association for the Advancement of Science (AAAS). 1993. *Benchmarks for science literacy.* New York: Oxford University Press.

Cosgrove, M., and R. Osborne. 1980. *Physical change.* LISP Working Paper 26, Science Education Research Unit, University of Waikato, Hamilton, New Zealand.

Driver, R., A. Squires, P. Rushworth, and V. Wood-Robinson. 1994. *Making sense of secondary science: Research into children's ideas.* London and New York: RoutledgeFalmer.

Keeley, P. 2005. *Science curriculum topic study: Bridging the gap between standards and practice.* Thousand Oaks, CA: Corwin Press.

National Research Council (NRC). 1996. *National science education standards.* Washington, DC: National Academy Press.

# Is It Matter?

Listed below is a list of things that are considered matter and things that are not considered matter. Put an X next to each of the things that you consider to be matter.

| | |
|---|---|
| _____ rocks | _____ salt |
| _____ baby powder | _____ Mars |
| _____ milk | _____ Jupiter |
| _____ air | _____ steam |
| _____ light | _____ rotten apples |
| _____ dust | _____ heat |
| _____ love | _____ sound waves |
| _____ cells | _____ water |
| _____ atoms | _____ bacteria |
| _____ fire | _____ oxygen |
| _____ smoke | _____ stars |

_____ gravity          _____ dissolved sugar

_____ magnetic force          _____ electricity

Explain your thinking. Describe the "rule" or reason you used to decide whether something is or is not matter.

_____

_____

_____

_____

_____

_____

_____

_____

# Is It Matter?

## Teacher Notes

## Purpose

The purpose of this assessment probe is to elicit students' ideas of what matter is. The probe is designed to determine whether students recognize forms of matter and can distinguish between things that are considered to be matter and things that are not (such as energy, forces, and emotions). The probe helps reveal what characteristics students use to decide if something is considered to be matter.

## Related Concepts

matter, energy, solids, liquids, gases, mass or weight

## Explanation

Items on the list considered to be matter are rocks, baby powder, milk, air, dust, cells, atoms, smoke, salt, Mars, Jupiter, steam, rotten apples, water, bacteria, oxygen, stars, and dissolved sugar. Responses to fire may vary depending on how the student thinks of fire. Fire may be considered matter or energy—the vaporized gases in the flame are matter but the light and heat emitted are energy. All matter is made up of particles (e.g., atoms or molecules); has weight and mass; takes up space (has volume); and exists in the forms of solid, liquid, gas, or plasma. In order to be considered matter, an object, material, or substance must meet these characteristics.

## Curricular and Instructional Considerations

### Elementary Students

By the end of the elementary grades, students frequently encounter the word *matter* in various topics such as states of matter, properties of matter, and changes in matter. National standards specifically target elementary grades as the time when students develop an understanding that matter exists as a solid, liquid, or gas and has properties that can be observed and measured, even with matter they cannot see, such as gases. The idea that air is a substance that we can feel and takes up space is a grade-level expectation in the national standards. Students develop a beginning notion of "stuff" as matter by examining the materials that make up objects. Energy is a more abstract idea at this stage. The probe is useful in determining what elementary students' initial ideas are about what constitutes matter and what criteria they use. It is especially helpful to determine if they recognize gases as something that fits with their conception of matter.

### Middle School Students

In middle school, students move from examining objects and materials to investigating substances. They start to develop a particulate model of matter that includes a beginning conception of atoms and molecules. The probe is useful in determining whether students link the ideas of observable and measurable properties (such as weight or mass, volume, size, and shape); existence in different states (solids, liq-

uids, gases); and tangible material or particles (substances, atoms, or molecules) to an explanation of whether something is considered to be matter. It can also be used to determine whether students are context-bound in their thinking about matter. This can happen if their prior experiences in learning about matter involved primarily solids and liquids or occurred primarily in a physical science context. The probe can alert teachers to the need to provide experiences with a variety of types of matter, including gases and living matter. It can also be used to provide feedback to the teacher on whether students distinguish between matter and forms of energy, informing instruction in energy-related concepts as well.

### High School Students

As the particulate notion of matter becomes more sophisticated in high school, students may still lack a complete idea of what constitutes matter. Although being able to define matter is not explicitly stated in the standards, developing a conception of matter is prerequisite to understanding several standards-based high school ideas, including flow of matter through ecosystems, states of matter, nature of energy, relationship between matter and energy, and behavior and characteristics of gases. This probe is useful in finding out if students retain their preconceptions about matter even after instruction.

### Administering the Probe

Make sure students are familiar with the items on the list. You may wish to remove items that

elementary students have little or no familiarity with. This probe can also be used as a card sort. In small groups, students can sort cards listing each item into two groups—those that are matter and those that are not. Listening carefully to students' discussions with each other as they sort can lend insight into their thinking. This probe can also be combined with "Ice Cubes in a Bag" (p. 49) and "Lemonade" (p. 55) since students' conservation reasoning is often linked to their conception of matter.

## Related Ideas in *National Science Education Standards* (NRC 1996)

· · · · · · · · · · · · · · · · · · · · · · · · · · · ·

### K–4 Properties of Objects and Materials

- Objects have many observable properties, including size, weight, and shape.
- Materials can exist in different states—solid, liquid, and gas.

### 9–12 Structure and Properties of Matter

- Matter is made up of minute particles called atoms.

## Related Ideas in *Benchmarks for Science Literacy* (AAAS 1993)

· · · · · · · · · · · · · · · · · · · · · · · · · · · ·

### K–2 Structure of Matter

- Objects can be described in terms of the materials they are made of and their physical properties.

### 3–5 The Earth

- Air is a substance that surrounds us, takes up space, and whose movement we feel as wind.

### 3–5 Structure of Matter

- Materials may be composed of parts that are too small to be seen without magnification.

### 6–8 Structure of Matter

- All matter is made up of atoms, which are far too small to see directly through a microscope.

## Related Research

- In a study conducted to find out the meaning students gave to the word *matter*, 20% of middle-school-age students described it as something tangible, meaning it could be handled and took up space. By age 16, 66% of students described it this way (Bouma, Brandt, and Sutton 1990).
- Student in grades 4–8 may think that everything that exists, including forms of energy, is matter. Alternatively, they may accept solids as matter but not liquids and gases (AAAS 1993).
- Having a correct conception of matter is necessary for students to understand ideas such as conservation of matter and weight/mass (AAAS 1993).
- Several studies have examined students' ideas about gases. These studies show that students have difficulty accepting the idea that air and other gases have material char-

acter and that they have weight or mass (Driver et al. 1994).

- Some students think of energy as an ingredient (Driver et al. 1994).

## Suggestions for Instruction and Assessment

- Knowing students' conception of matter is prerequisite to designing instruction around several matter-related concepts.

- Do not assume that students know what matter is when you use the term. Start with a familiar, operative word, such as *stuff*, until students are ready to use the scientific word *matter*. Be aware that providing a definition such as "matter is anything that has mass and occupies space" is meaningless to students if they don't know what mass and volume are.

- Provide students with experiences that demonstrate (a) all three states of matter, particularly gases, when learning about matter and its properties; (b) physical and chemical changes; (c) conservation of matter; (d) measurement of properties; (e) mass and volume relationships; (f) atoms as building blocks; and (g) classifying matter as elements, compounds, and mixtures.

- Be explicit in defining what matter is, starting with student-developed operational definitions and refining definitions to become more scientific as students gain additional knowledge. Use the operational and scientific definition to provide examples of things that are not matter.

- Develop a "rule" with students for deter-

mining what matter is and have students use the rule to justify ideas about whether something is matter.

- Have students determine weight or mass (if they are familiar with the term *mass*) of seemingly "weightless" materials, such as gases and powders.

- Have students demonstrate what it means to "take up space" with solids, liquids, and gases. Show evidence for the existence of gases and how they take up space, such as feeling the wind, blowing up a balloon, or turning a glass with a tissue stuffed in it upside down in water. Test the idea on things that do not take up space (light, sound).

- Teach and assess the idea of matter in multiple contexts, not just physical science (living matter, Earth materials, and matter in space).

- Sophisticated ideas that may contradict a basic notion of matter such as a particle model of light and light having mass should wait until high school when students are ready to comprehend the matter and energy relationship and understand how a particle of light (photon) differs from a particle of matter.

## Related NSTA Science Store Publications and Journal Articles

Abell, S., M. Anderson, D. Ruth, and N. Sattler. 1996. What's the matter? Studying the concept of matter in middle school. *Science Scope* (Sept.): 18–21.

Deters, K. 2004. Inquiry in the chemistry classroom. *The Science Teacher* (Dec.): 42–45.

Driver, R., A. Squires, P. Rushworth, and V. Wood-Robinson. 1994. *Making sense of secondary science: Research into children's ideas.* London and New York: RoutledgeFalmer.

Keeley, P. 2005. *Science curriculum topic study: Bridging the gap between standards and practice.* Thousand Oaks, CA: Corwin Press.

Keeley, P., F. Eberle, and L. Farrin. 2005. Formative assessment probes: Uncovering students' ideas in science. *Science Scope* (Jan.): 18–21.

Ontario Science Centre. 1995. *Solids, liquids, and gases.* Tonawanda, NY: Kids Can Press.

Stepans, J. 2003. *Targeting students' science misconceptions: Physical science concepts using the conceptual change model.* (See section on matter.) Tampa, FL: Showboard.

## References

American Association for the Advancement of Science (AAAS). 1993. *Benchmarks for science literacy.* New York: Oxford University Press.

Bouma, H., I. Brandt, and C. Sutton. 1990. *Words as tools in science lessons.* Amsterdam: University of Amsterdam.

Driver, R., A. Squires, P. Rushworth, and V. Wood-Robinson. 1994. *Making sense of secondary science: Research into children's ideas.* London and New York: RoutledgeFalmer.

Keeley, P. 2005. *Science curriculum topic study: Bridging the gap between standards and practice.* Thousand Oaks, CA: Corwin Press.

National Research Council (NRC). 1996. *National science education standards.* Washington, DC: National Academy Press.

### Related Curriculum Topic Study Guides
(Keeley 2005)
"Properties of Matter"
"Particulate Nature of Matter"
"States of Matter"

# Is It Made of Molecules?

Put an X next to the things on the list that are made up of one or more molecules.

| | |
|---|---|
| _____ bread | _____ DNA |
| _____ protons | _____ cell membrane |
| _____ water | _____ cloud |
| _____ atomic nucleus | _____ oil |
| _____ brain cell | _____ worm |
| _____ milk | _____ protein |
| _____ egg | _____ sugar |
| _____ atom | _____ flower |

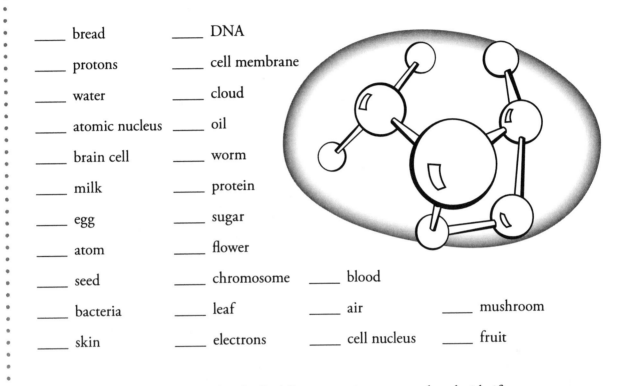

| | | | |
|---|---|---|---|
| _____ seed | _____ chromosome | _____ blood | |
| _____ bacteria | _____ leaf | _____ air | _____ mushroom |
| _____ skin | _____ electrons | _____ cell nucleus | _____ fruit |

Explain your thinking. Describe the "rule" or reasoning you used to decide if something was made of molecules.

_____

_____

_____

_____

_____

_____

_____

# Is It Made of Molecules?

## Teacher Notes

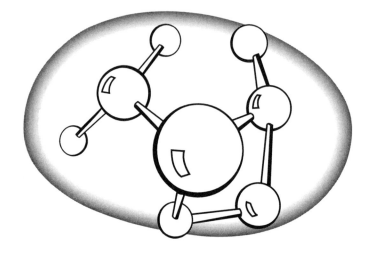

## Purpose

The purpose of this assessment probe is to elicit students' ideas about molecules. The probe is designed to find out whether students recognize that various examples of both physical and biological matter, ranging from objects to materials, can be made of molecules. It also helps determine whether students recognize a hierarchy of structure in the composition of matter ranging from molecules to single atoms to parts of an atom.

## Related Concepts

atoms, molecules, matter

## Explanation

A molecule is formed when two or more atoms join together by sharing electrons to form a larger particle. Most gases and liquids at ordinary temperatures are made of molecules. Not all matter is made of molecules. Matter can also exist as metals and ionic crystalline lattice structures, depending how the bonds between atoms form. Nonmolecular substances are not included in the list since the assessment probe is not asking students to distinguish between ways atoms bond to form substances. Carbon forms organic molecules and a large array of organic molecules make up living or once-living material. All the forms of matter on this list except for protons, atoms, electrons, and atomic nucleus are made up of molecules. There is a hierarchy of arrangement from particles and parts that make up an atom to atoms to single molecules to substances. Protons, electrons, and an atomic nucleus are particles that make

up an atom, which can be part of a molecule. Even though these are parts that make up a molecule, the reverse is not true. A molecule does not make up atoms, electrons, protons, or an atomic nucleus.

## Curricular and Instructional Considerations

### Elementary Students

Students at this grade level can understand the idea that matter is made up of smaller parts. They may use the word *molecules* or may have heard it used, but they lack a sophisticated model of matter to explain what molecules are and how atoms or parts of an atom relate to the idea of molecules. This assessment probe may be modified for upper elementary students by changing the context to "what things on the list are made up of smaller parts" and adding other familiar objects to replace atoms and parts of atoms.

### Middle School Students

Middle school is a time when students begin to develop a particulate notion of matter to understand atoms, molecules, and compounds. When students are first introduced to atoms they are not able to distinguish between atoms and molecules. Later they begin to understand that atoms combine to form molecules in familiar compounds like water. There is a danger that students may become context-bound. If they learn about compounds and molecules in physical science using primarily examples such as water, carbon dioxide, or table sugar, they

may fail to realize that materials like food, cells, and others with a biological origin are also made of molecules. The probe is useful in determining the variety of contexts where students can use the idea of molecules. Depending on the developmental level of the students, some may believe that atoms are the smallest components of a substance and therefore are not made up of molecules. Since atoms make up molecules, they are not made of molecules themselves, even though they are matter. This distinction reflects a more complex level of understanding about matter, which is appropriate at or above the middle school level. Although students may not understand the parts of an atom at this grade level, it is likely they have heard of them. The probe may be useful in uncovering their early conceptions about these parts in relation to a molecule.

### High School Students

In high school the same hierarchical misconceptions may persist, even though this is a time when parts of an atom are a grade-level expectation in the national standards. Context is also a factor. In biology students learn about various molecules necessary for life but may fail to recognize that cells and cell structures are made up of molecules. The national standards include several ideas that use the concept of molecules; therefore, this probe is useful in determining if students have a conception of molecular matter.

### Administering the Probe

This probe asks for a fairly sophisticated

**SCiLINKS**
THE WORLD'S A CLICK AWAY

Topic: Atoms/Molecules
Go to: *www.scilinks.org*
Code: USIS88

understanding of matter, beyond just whether something is matter or not. The probe can be modified to include only substances, objects, and materials that students may have familiarity with; you can have students cross off the items on the list they are unfamiliar with. This probe can also be used as a card sort. In small groups, students can sort cards into two groups—items that are made up of molecules and those that are not. Listening carefully to students' discussions with each other as they sort can lend insight into their thinking. This probe can be used in conjunction with other probes such as "Is It Matter?" (p. 79) to learn if students have similar difficulties with fundamental conceptions of matter.

## Related Ideas in *National Science Education Standards* (NRC 1996)

### 5–8 Properties and Changes in Properties in Matter

- There are more than 100 elements that combine in a multitude of ways to produce compounds, which account for the living and nonliving substances that we encounter.

### 9–12 Structure and Properties of Matter

★ Matter is made of minute particles called atoms, and atoms are composed of even smaller components. Each atom has a positively charged nucleus surrounded by

negatively charged electrons.

★ The atom's nucleus is composed of protons and neutrons.

★ Atoms may be bonded together into molecules or crystalline solids.

★ Carbon atoms can bond to one another in chains, rings, and branching networks to form a variety of structures, including synthetic polymers, oils, and the large molecules essential to life.

### 9–12 The Cell

★ Inside the cell is a concentrated mixture of thousands of different molecules that form a variety of specialized structures that carry out cell functions.

- Food molecules taken into cells react to provide the chemical constituents needed to synthesize other molecules.

## Related Ideas in *Benchmarks for Science Literacy* (AAAS 1993)

### 3–5 Structure of Matter

- Materials may be composed of parts that are too small to be seen without magnification.

### 6–8 Structure of Matter

★ All matter is made up of atoms. Atoms may stick together in well-defined molecules.

### 6–8 Flow of Matter and Energy

- Food provides molecules that serve as fuel and building material for all organisms.

---

★ Indicates a strong match between the ideas elicited by the probe and a national standard's learning goal.

### 9–12 Structure of Matter

- Atoms are made of a positive nucleus surrounded by negative electrons.
- The nucleus, a tiny fraction of the volume of an atom, is composed of protons and neutrons.
- ★ Atoms often join with one another in various combinations in distinct molecules or in repeating three-dimensional crystal patterns.

### 9–12 The Cell

- ★ The work of the cell is carried out by the many different types of molecules it assembles, mostly proteins.
- ★ Carbon atoms can easily bond to several other carbon atoms in chains and rings to form large and complex molecules.

## Related Research

- A correct understanding of a single, a collection, or combination of atoms is directly related to the concept of molecules (Stavy and Tirosh 2000).
- Understanding how molecules make up other small objects such as cells may be tied to difficulty students have understanding how small something is (Driver et al. 1994).
- Arnold (1983) showed how students confuse cells with molecules. When he asked students ages 14–15 to indicate whether certain things were made up of cells and/ or molecules, things that were living or once living were designated as being made of cells but not molecules. Even molecules studied in biology such as carbohydrates

and proteins were thought to be made up of cells, not molecules. Arnold concluded that students seem to confine the concept of a molecule to contexts encountered in physical science classes or units.

- Even though students may indicate they know about cells, they may say that living systems are made of cells not molecules, because students often only associate molecules with physical science (NRC 1996).

## Suggestions for Instruction and Assessment

- Help students understand that molecules make up a variety of materials, beyond the examples they encounter in a physical science context, including atmospheric and biological materials and objects. Explicitly address the idea that living and once-living things are composed of organic molecules.
- Develop ideas of hierarchy from parts of an atom to atoms to molecules to substances to objects and materials. Explicitly address the idea that cells and other biological materials contain substances made up of molecules.
- Teach and use ideas of matter (living matter, Earth materials, chemical material, and matter in space) in multiple contexts, not just physical science.
- Visual models help students develop a hierarchical idea of atomic particles, the nucleus of an atom, atoms, molecules, and substances. Models show that each part includes the preceding part, but the reverse order does not apply.

---

★ Indicates a strong match between the ideas elicited by the probe and a national standard's learning goal.

## Related NSTA Science Store Publications and NSTA Journal Articles

American Association for the Advancement of Science (AAAS). 2001. *Atlas of science literacy.* (See "Atoms and Molecules," pp. 54–55, "Flow of Matter in Ecosystems," pp. 76–77, "Cells and Organs," pp. 74–75.) New York: Oxford University Press.

Driver, R., A. Squires, P. Rushworth, and V. Wood-Robinson. 1994. *Making sense of secondary science: Research into children's ideas.* London and New York: RoutledgeFalmer.

Hitt, A., and J. Townsend. 2004. Models that matter. *The Science Teacher* (Mar.): 29–31.

Keeley, P. 2005. *Science curriculum topic study: Bridging the gap between standards and practice.* Thousand Oaks, CA: Corwin Press.

Stepans, J. 2003. *Targeting students' science misconceptions: Physical science concepts using the conceptual change model.* (See section on recent concepts). Tampa, FL: Showboard.

## References

American Association for the Advancement of Science (AAAS). 1993. *Benchmarks for science literacy.* New York: Oxford University Press.

Arnold, B. 1983. Beware the molecell! *Biology Newsletter* (Aberdeen College of Education) 42: 2–6.

Driver, R., A. Squires, P. Rushworth, and V. Wood-Robinson. 1994. *Making sense of secondary science: Research into children's ideas.* London and New York: RoutledgeFalmer.

Keeley, P. 2005. *Science curriculum topic study: Bridging the gap between standards and practice.* Thousand Oaks, CA: Corwin Press.

National Research Council (NRC). 1996. *National science education standards.* Washington, DC. National Academy Press.

Stavy, R., and D. Tirosh. 2000. *How students (mis-) understand science and mathematics: Intuitive rules.* New York: Teachers College Press.

### Related Curriculum Topic Study Guides

(Keeley 2005)

"Particulate Nature of Matter (Atoms and Molecules)"

"Chemistry of Life"

"Chemical Bonding"

# The Rusty Nails

You have four nails made of pure iron. You record the total mass of the four dry nails. The four nails are put in a moist, open dish and exposed to the air over several weeks. Weeks later you notice the nails are covered with rust. You let the nails dry completely and record the total mass of the rusted nails. You are very careful not to let any of the rust fall off the nails as you weigh them.

What do you predict will happen to the mass of the nails? Circle your prediction.

**A** The mass of the dry, rusted nails will be more than the mass of the dry nails before they rusted.

**B** The mass of the dry, rusted nails will be less than the mass of the dry nails before they rusted.

**C** The mass of the dry, rusted nails will be the same as the mass of the dry nails before they rusted.

Describe your thinking. Provide an explanation for your answer.

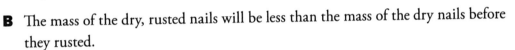

_____

_____

_____

_____

_____

_____

_____

_____

# The Rusty Nails

## Teacher Notes

## Purpose

The purpose of this assessment probe is to elicit students' ideas about a common chemical change. The task is designed to find out if students think rusting is a change in which mass decreases, due to an intuitive notion of rusting as being similar to a decay process.

## Related Concepts

chemical change, oxidation, mass or weight

## Explanation

The best response is A. Rusting is an example of oxidation—a chemical change in which electrons from the iron atoms are transferred to the oxygen atoms, resulting in the formation of a new compound. The oxygen in the air chemically combines with the iron. As a result

the additional mass from the oxygen is added to the mass of the nail to form a new compound, iron oxide. Although the appearance of the nail makes it look as if it is "breaking down," it is actually gaining mass as it changes from iron to iron oxide. Some students may apply conservation reasoning to explain that the mass does not change. This would be true if the nails were kept in a closed system and the mass determined was that of the total system. The probe specifically states the nails were placed in an open dish.

## Curricular and Instructional Considerations

### Elementary Students

Elementary students begin developing ideas

about changes in objects and materials. They can recognize rust as a change in the appearance of the nail. Upper elementary students begin distinguishing between physical and chemical changes based on observation of changes in properties. Rust is often used as an example of a chemical change. This probe may be useful in determining students' early notions of rusting, particularly whether they view rusting as a "decomposing" process. However, the chemical details are too sophisticated to be addressed at this age level.

### Middle School Students

Middle school is the time when students link ideas about chemical change with formation of compounds. Rust is commonly used as an example of a chemical change that results in a new compound with properties that differ from the original substance. These basic ideas about chemical change are included as grade-level expectations in the national standards. However, the mechanism of that change, explained by the interaction between iron and oxygen atoms, is a more sophisticated idea developed in high school. The probe is useful in determining students' initial ideas about what rust and the rusting process are. The appearance of the rusty nail may influence students' thinking that the nail is breaking down and losing mass. Knowing the ideas students hold prior to learning that oxygen combines with iron during the rusting process is useful in designing learning experiences that challenge their intuitive notions influenced by observation.

### High School Students

Students at this grade level make a transition from a basic understanding of types of chemical changes, including the formation of compounds when two elements are chemically combined, to understanding the mechanism for the combination. Students at this level are more likely to understand why the mass increases by learning about the interaction between the atoms of the two substances and about the difference between synthesis and decomposition reactions. The probe is useful in determining whether students still hold on to preconceived ideas about rusting, even after they have received middle school instruction targeted toward the idea that oxygen combines with the iron to form rust.

**Topic: Oxidation**
**Go to: www.scilinks.org**
**Code: USIS93**

### Administering the Probe

Be sure students understand that the nails are not contained in a closed system. The nails are in an open dish. If students have experienced prior conservation of matter probes, they may automatically think that mass does not change. Some students think the rust falls off, resulting in less mass. Emphasize that the nail and all of its rust, including any rust that falls off, are weighed. You may wish to show students actual nails or photographs—in either case, comparing four clean iron nails (not galvanized) and four nails that have rusted.

## Related Ideas in *National Science Education Standards* (NRC 1996)

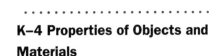

### K–4 Properties of Objects and Materials

- Objects have many observable properties, including size, weight, shape, color, temperature, and the ability to react with other substances.

### 5–8 Properties and Changes in Properties of Matter

- Substances react chemically in characteristic ways with other substances to form new substances (compounds) with different characteristic properties. In chemical reactions, the total mass is conserved.

### 9–12 Structure and Properties of Matter

- Chemical reactions occur all around us.
- ★ A large number of important reactions involve the transfer of either electrons (oxidation/reduction reactions) or hydrogen ions (acid/base reactions) between reacting ions, molecules, or atoms.

## Related Ideas in *Benchmarks for Science Literacy* (AAAS 1993)

### K–2 Structure of Matter

- Objects can be described in terms of the materials they are made of (e.g., clay, cloth, paper) and their physical properties (e.g., color, size, shape, weight, texture, flexibility).
- Things can be done to materials to change some of their properties, but not all materials respond the same way to what is done to them.

### 3–5 Structure of Matter

- When a new material is made by combining two or more materials, it has properties that are different from the original materials.

### 6–8 Structure of Matter

- Because most elements tend to combine with others, few elements are found in their pure form.
- ★ An especially important kind of reaction between substances involves combination of oxygen with something else, as in burning or rusting.

### 9–12 Structure of Matter

- Atoms often join with one another in various combinations in distinct molecules or in repeating three-dimensional crystal patterns. An enormous variety of biological, chemical, and physical phenomena can be explained by changes in the arrangement and motion of atoms and molecules.

## Related Research

- Middle and high school students' ideas about chemical change tend to be dominated by the obvious features of the change (AAAS 1993). For example, students are likely to think that when something rusts it weighs less because it looks as if parts of the metal are being "eaten away" or the powdery rust is less substantive than the iron (Driver 1985).
- Some students describe rust as a type of mold (Driver et al. 1994).

---

★ Indicates a strong match between the ideas elicited by the probe and a national standard's learning goal.

- Some students think that rust comes from the nail itself. Some students explain that it is already under the surface of the nail and is exposed during the rusting process (Driver et al. 1994).

- Students' everyday experience with rusting often involves iron getting wet. Consequently students are likely to think that rusting happens as a result of the water eating away at the metal, rather than its being an interaction with oxygen in the air (Driver et al. 1994).

- In a survey conducted of English 15-year-old students, one-third said the rusty nail would weigh less, one-third said more, and one-third said it would stay the same. Of these students, just over 10% of those studying chemistry said the mass would increase because the mass of the rust is added to the mass of the nail. There was no indication from their response that the iron in the nail was involved in the formation of rust. Others who understood the reaction explained that the mass would not change because oxygen doesn't weigh anything (Driver 1985).

- Some students use the "taught" ideas about oxidation but adapt them to their intuitive notions of rusting using reasoning such as "the oxygen dissolves some of the iron" (Driver 1985).

## Suggestions for Instruction and Assessment

- This probe can be followed up as an inquiry-based investigation that uses nongalvanized nails. Ask the question, encourage students to commit to a prediction, and then test it. The dissonance involved in discovering that the mass increases is followed by opportunities for students to resolve the dissonance by discussing where the additional mass came from.

- Help students use the idea of change in mass as an explanation for chemical change. Since the mass of the nail increases during rusting, help students use this phenomenon as evidence that other matter was added to the nail during the change.

- Explicitly address the idea that gases such as oxygen have perceptible mass.

- If middle or high school students think of rust as a type of "mold" that decomposes metal, compare the biological process of decomposition with the chemical process of oxidation to help students recognize the difference.

- Help students draw parallels between other types of chemical change that involve combination with oxygen, such as combustion reactions, to rusting.

- *Safety Note:* Rusty nails by themselves, in a dish, do not present a safety hazard. If students handle the nails, however, have them wash their hands afterwards.

## Related NSTA Science Store Publications and NSTA Journal Articles

American Association for the Advancement of Science (AAAS). 2001. *Atlas of science literacy.* (See "Chemical Reactions," pp. 60–61.) New York: Oxford University Press.

Driver, R., A. Squires, P. Rushworth, and V. Wood-Robinson. 1994. *Making sense of secondary science: Research into children's ideas.* London and New York: RoutledgeFalmer.

Heiserman, D. L. 1992. *Exploring chemical elements and their compounds.* New York: TAB Books.

Keeley, P. 2005. *Science curriculum topic study: Bridging the gap between standards and practice.* Thousand Oaks, CA: Corwin Press.

Stepans, J. 2003. *Targeting students' science misconceptions: Physical science concepts using the conceptual change model.* (See section on recent concepts.) Tampa, FL: Showboard.

Volkmann, M., and S. Abell. 2003. Rethinking laboratories. *The Science Teacher* (Sept.): 38–41.

**Related Curriculum Topic Study Guide**
(Keeley 2005)
"Chemical Properties and Change"

## References

American Association for the Advancement of Science (AAAS). 1993. *Benchmarks for science literacy.* New York: Oxford University Press.

Driver, R. 1985. Beyond appearances: The conservation of matter. In *Children's ideas in science,* eds. R. Driver, E. Guesne, and A. Tiberghien. Milton Keynes, UK: Open University Press.

Driver, R., A. Squires, P. Rushworth, and V. Wood-Robinson. 1994. *Making sense of secondary science: Research into children's ideas.* London and New York: RoutledgeFalmer.

Keeley, P. 2005. *Science curriculum topic study: Bridging the gap between standards and practice.* Thousand Oaks, CA: Corwin Press.

National Research Council (NRC). 1996. *National science education standards.* Washington, DC: National Academy Press.

# Talking About Gravity

Two friends were talking about gravity.

Ben said, "Gravity needs an atmosphere or air. If there is no air or atmosphere, there will be no gravity."

Kelly said, "Gravity doesn't need an atmosphere or air. If there is no air or atmosphere, there will still be gravity."

Which friend do you agree with? _____

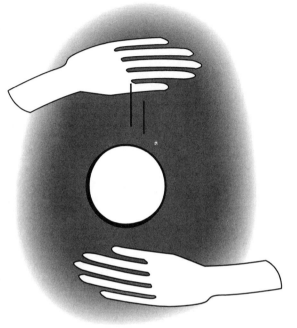

Describe your thinking. Explain why you agree with one friend and disagree with the other.

_____

_____

_____

_____

_____

_____

_____

_____

_____

_____

_____

_____

_____

# Talking About Gravity

## Teacher Notes

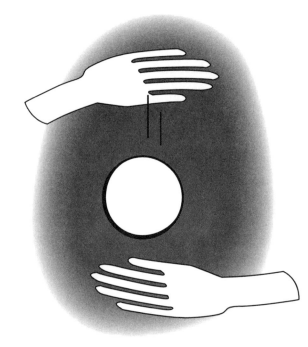

### Purpose

The purpose of this assessment probe is to elicit students' ideas about gravity. The probe is designed to determine whether students recognize that gravity is a universal force that exists everywhere in space, regardless of whether air is present.

### Related Concept

gravity

### Explanation

Gravity is a universal attraction between any two objects with mass. Every object in the universe is affected by the force of gravity. The two factors that affect the magnitude of the force of gravity are the mass of the attracted objects and the distance between them. The greater the masses the greater the gravitational force between two objects. The greater the distance between two objects, the less the gravitational force between them. Each object with mass in the universe is attracted to all other objects, regardless of size or distance. Whether you are on the Moon, Earth, or deep in outer space, gravity is present. Air or an atmosphere is not needed for gravity.

## Curricular and Instructional Considerations

### Elementary Students

By the end of the elementary grades, most students know that things fall toward the Earth, have heard the word *gravity*, and have begun to understand that gravity pulls things toward the Earth. They have seen videos of astronauts in space and have heard the misuse of terms in the media such as *zero gravity* and *weightlessness*. These images and terms may result in students formulating early ideas that gravity affects objects on Earth but not in space, particularly since their experiences and contexts deal with terrestrial gravity. It is not until middle school when students begin to learn about celestial gravity. However, this probe is useful in determining whether students have already formed preconceptions about gravity prior to formal instruction at the appropriate grade level.

### Middle School Students

In middle school, students expand on their basic elementary grade knowledge of gravity to include the idea of gravity in space. They develop the idea of a gravitational force that is center-directed, affects all objects, and depends on objects' mass and distance. They develop a notion of weight as being distinct from mass. This is also a time when students learn about moons that lack an atmosphere or have a very thin atmosphere, and hear references to astronauts being "weightless" in space. The probe is useful in determining if students rec-

ognize gravity as being universal or confuse it with ideas such as air needing to be present.

### High School Students

In high school, students continue to build more sophisticated understandings about gravity by using proportional relationships to explain increases or decreases in gravitational attraction. Even though students may quantitatively understand gravitational force, there is a likelihood that they may hold on to their preconceived ideas about air being necessary. This may be compounded by confusing air pressure with gravity. The probe is useful in uncovering misconceptions that may go unnoticed during formal instruction.

### Administering the Probe

Encourage students to explain in detail the evidence or justification for their thinking.

## Related Ideas in *National Science Education Standards* (NRC 1996)

### K–4 Position and Motion of Objects

- The position and motion of objects can be changed by pushing or pulling. The size of the change is related to the strength of the push or pull.

### 5–8 Earth in the Solar System

★ Gravity is the force that keeps planets in orbit around the Sun and governs the rest of the motion in the solar system. Gravity

Topic: Gravity
Go to: *www.scilinks.org*
Code: USIS99

---

★ Indicates a strong match between the ideas elicited by the probe and a national standard's learning goal.

alone holds us to the Earth's surface and explains the phenomena of the tides.

### 9–12 Motions and Forces

★ Gravitation is the universal force that each mass exerts on any other mass. The strength of the gravitational attractive force between two masses is proportional to the masses and inversely proportional to the square of the distance between them.

## Related Ideas in *Benchmarks for Science Literacy* (AAAS 1993)

### K–2 Forces of Nature

• Things near to the Earth fall to the ground unless something holds them up.

### 3–5 Forces of Nature

• The Earth's gravity pulls any objects toward it without touching it.

### 6–8 The Earth

• Everything on or anywhere near the Earth is pulled toward the Earth's center by gravitational force.

### 6–8 Forces of Nature

★ Every object exerts gravitational force on every other object. The force depends on how much mass the objects have and on how far apart they are. The force is hard to detect unless one of the objects has a lot of mass.

• The Sun's gravitational pull holds the Earth and other planets in their orbits, just as

the planets' gravitational pull keeps their moons in orbit around them.

### 9–12 Forces of Nature

• Gravitational force is an attraction between masses. The strength of the force is proportional to the masses and weakens rapidly with increasing distance between them.

## Related Research

• Students' confusion about air being necessary for gravity may be related to their view of weight as a force. Studies by Ruggiero et al. (1985) found that some students think air is the force that results in weight. They found that the idea that air must be present for gravity to act was widespread among middle school students they sampled.

• Relating gravity to air provides insight into students' ideas about gravity being something that resides outside of objects rather than all objects exerting gravitational pull (Driver et al. 1994).

• Many researchers acknowledge that misconceptions about the cause of gravity persist even after high school physics instruction. Students' ideas can change with specially designed instruction (AAAS 1993).

• Some students describe a "holding" idea that an atmosphere holds gravity in (Driver et al. 1994).

• Some students think Earth's magnetism and spin cause gravity (Driver et al. 1994).

• Some studies of middle and high school students show that very few believe all

---

★ Indicates a strong match between the ideas elicited by the probe and a national standard's learning goal.

objects exert a gravitational force (Driver et al. 1994).

## Suggestions for Instruction and Assessment

• When developing the idea that there are two factors that affect gravity—mass and distance—explicitly point out that air or an atmosphere is not a factor and provide evidence to prove it using phenomena such as men walking on the Moon (if there were no gravity, they couldn't stay on the surface).

• Confront students' ideas about gravity and air by placing an object in a vacuum jar and removing all the air. Ask students to predict what would happen to the object if there were no gravity acting on it as a result of removing all the air from the jar. Perform the demonstration and ask students if they want to revise their ideas based on the evidence. If students still maintain that air is necessary, show the NASA Apollo video of astronauts dropping objects on the Moon, where there is no air (or just a bare hint of an atmosphere). There are also videos available that show feathers and heavy balls falling in a vacuum tube. Without air resistance they fall at the same rate as gravity pulls on both.

• Help students understand that gravity keeps an atmosphere in place and not vice versa. Use planets as an example of large objects exerting a stronger gravitational pull, in this case on an atmosphere. Contrast it with smaller objects, like the Moon, not being large enough to exert a gravitational pull that would maintain a sufficient atmosphere.

• Be aware that terms used in the media like *weightless* and *zero gravity* perpetuate the idea that there is no gravity in some places. Use the term *microgravity* when referring to a small gravitational effect.

• Demonstrate what is actually happening when it appears as if astronauts are weightless and "floating" inside a space shuttle by using diagrams to show that astronauts are actually in free fall around the Earth.

## Related NSTA Science Store Publications and NSTA Journal Articles

American Association for the Advancement of Science. 2001. *Atlas of science literacy.* (See "Gravity," pp. 42–43.) New York: Oxford University Press.

Bar, V., C. Sneider, and N. Martimbeau. 1997. Is there gravity in space? *Science and Children* (Apr.): 38–43.

Driver, R., A. Squires, P. Rushworth, and V. Wood-Robinson. 1994. *Making sense of secondary science: Research into children's ideas.* London and New York: RoutledgeFalmer.

Keeley, P. 2005. *Science curriculum topic study: Bridging the gap between standards and practice.* Thousand Oaks, CA: Corwin Press.

Nelson, G. 2004. What is gravity? *Science and Children* (Sept.): 22–23.

Robertson, W. 2003. *Force and motion: Stop faking it! Finally understanding science so you can teach it.* Arlington, VA: NSTA Press.

Sneider, C. 2003. Examining students' work. In *Everyday assessment in the science classroom*, eds. J. M. Atkin and J. E. Coffey, 27–40. Arlington, VA: NSTA Press.

**Related Curriculum Topic Study Guides**
(Keeley 2005)
"Gravity in Space"
"Gravitational Force"

## References

American Association for the Advancement of Science (AAAS). 1993. *Benchmarks for science literacy.* New York: Oxford University Press.

Driver, R., A. Squires, P. Rushworth, and V. Wood-Robinson. 1994. *Making sense of secondary science: Research into children's ideas.* London and New York: RoutledgeFalmer.

Keeley, P. 2005. *Science curriculum topic study: Bridging the gap between standards and practice.* Thousand Oaks, CA: Corwin Press.

National Research Council (NRC). 1996. *National science education standards.* Washington, DC: National Academy Press.

Ruggiero, S., A. Cartielli, F. Dupre, and M. Vincentini-Missoni. 1985. Weight, gravity, and air pressure: Mental representations by Italian middle-school pupils. *European Journal of Science Education* 7(2): 181–194.

# The Mitten Problem

Sarah's science class is investigating heat energy. They wonder what would happen to the temperature reading on a thermometer if they put the thermometer inside a mitten.

Sarah's group obtained two thermometers and a mitten. They put one thermometer inside the mitten and the other thermometer on the table next to the mitten. An hour later they compared the readings on the two thermometers. The temperature inside the room remained the same during their experiment.

What do you think Sarah's group will discover from their investigation? Circle the response that best matches your thinking.

**A** The thermometer inside the mitten will have a lower temperature reading than the thermometer on the table.

**B** The thermometer inside the mitten will have a higher temperature reading than the thermometer on the table.

**C** Both thermometers will have the same temperature reading.

Describe your thinking. Provide an explanation for your answer.

_____

_____

_____

_____

_____

# The Mitten Problem

## Teacher Notes

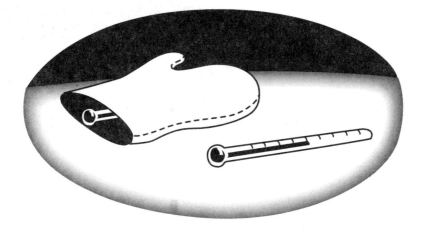

## Purpose

The purpose of this assessment probe is to elicit students' ideas about sources of heat energy. The probe is designed to find out whether students believe an insulating object, like a mitten, produces its own heat. Their explanations reveal whether they can differentiate between a heat source and an object affected by a heat source.

## Related Concepts

heat, energy, temperature

## Explanation

The best response is C. The temperature readings inside the mitten and outside the mitten will be the same. Heat describes the energy that is transferred between two interacting systems at different temperatures. A heat source can produce its own heat energy or it may simply be an object that is at a higher temperature than the surroundings. The mitten in this case does not produce its own heat energy, and it did not have a higher starting temperature to begin with when the thermometer was inserted. The mitten is an insulator that keeps heat, generated by the human body and transferred to the surrounding air, from leaving the mitten as quickly as it leaves a bare hand. The mitten, which is an insulator, slows down the transfer of heat energy to the surrounding environment outside the mitten. If there is no source of additional heat energy inside the mitten, the mitten will have the same temperature as its ambient surroundings. Temperature is closely related to the measure of the average kinetic energy of molecules and atoms. During this experiment there is nothing to significantly cause the average motion of the atoms and molecules of the mitten or the air inside it to increase. The temperature in the room remained the same throughout the experiment. Therefore the temperature will most likely remain the same inside the mitten as outside the mitten.

## Curricular and Instructional Considerations

### Elementary Students

Students experiment with heat in the elementary grades and begin to understand that heat-related phenomena can be observed, measured, and controlled in various ways. The concept of energy is complex, yet students develop intuitive notions about energy, including heat. Basic ideas at this level are observational. Grade-level expectations in the national standards include development of the idea of various ways heat is produced, that heat moves from warmer objects to cooler ones, and that there are ways to reduce heat loss. Students at this level do not distinguish between the words *heat* and *temperature,* and this may confound their understanding of what heat is and how it travels. This probe is useful in determining early ideas about heat transfer and whether students think insulating objects, such as mittens, coats, and blankets, generate their own heat.

### Middle School Students

Students' understandings about heat will build on their K–4 experiences. They become familiar with the ideas that energy is an important property of substances and that many changes involve energy transfer in the form of heat. However, students still have many misconceptions about heat and where it comes from. Confusion between concepts of temperature, heat, energy transfer, and a heat source is common at this level and focusing on transformations may help them address their naive ideas. The idea that heat results from the motion of molecules is a grade-level expectation in the middle and high school standards. However, this is still an abstract notion. The probe is useful in determining if students still persist in their preconceptions about temperature, energy, and non-heat-generating objects.

### High School Students

Heat and temperature ideas become more complex at this age. Yet, students may still hold onto ideas they had in elementary grades as well as fail to distinguish between the use of the words *heat* and *temperature.* High school students build on their experiences with energy transfer in the middle grades to investigate heat quantitatively by measuring variables such as temperature change and kinetic energy (NRC 1996). Students can experience and analyze a wide variety of actions that give off heat and understand that the mitten prevents some heat given off by the body from dissipating into the environment outside the mitten. However, misconceptions about heat sources may still persist and be uncovered through use of this probe.

## Administering the Probe

You may wish to use props to model the idea that the mitten with the thermometer inside and the thermometer on the table are exposed to the same ambient conditions. This probe may be combined with "Objects and Temperature" (p. 109) to further probe for students' ideas about heat transfer and temperature.

## Related Ideas in *National Science Education Standards* (NRC 1996)

. . . . . . . . . . . . . . . . . . . . . . . . . . . .

### K–4 Light, Heat, Electricity, and Magnetism

- Heat can be produced in many ways, such as burning, rubbing, or mixing one substance with another. Heat can move from one object to another by conduction.

### 5–8 Transfer of Energy

- Energy is a property of many substances and is associated with heat, light, electricity, mechanical motion, sound, nuclei, and the nature of a chemical. Energy is transferred in many ways.
- ★ Heat moves in predictable ways, flowing from warmer objects to cooler ones, until both reach the same temperature.

### 9–12 Conservation of Energy and the Increase in Disorder

- Heat consists of random motion and the vibrations of atoms, molecules, and ions. The higher the temperature, the greater the atomic or molecular motion.

## Related Ideas in *Benchmarks for Science Literacy* (AAAS 1993)

. . . . . . . . . . . . . . . . . . . . . . . . . . . .

### 3–5 Energy Transformation

- Heat is produced by mechanical and electrical machines and any time one thing rubs up against another.
- When warmer things are put with cooler ones, the warm ones lose heat and the cool ones gain it until they are all at the same temperature.
- ★ Poor conductors can reduce heat loss.

### 6–8 Energy Transformation

- Energy cannot be created or destroyed, but only changed from one form into another.
- ★ Energy appears in different forms. Heat energy is in the disorderly motion of molecules.

### 9–12 Energy Transformation

- Heat energy in a material consists of the disordered motions of its atoms or molecules.
- Transformations of energy usually produce some energy in the form of heat, which spreads around by radiation or conduction into cooler places.

## Related Research

- Although the operational distinction between temperature and heat can be fairly well understood after careful instruction, research with high school students indicates that the idea that heat is the energy of random motion and vibrating molecules is difficult for students to understand (NRC 1996).

---

★ Indicates a strong match between the ideas elicited by the probe and a national standard's learning goal.

Topic: Heat/Temperature
Go to: *www.scilinks.org*
Code: USIS107

- Heat energy is an unexpectedly difficult concept for students to grasp, as temperature is often mistaken as heat. Most children can't distinguish between heat and temperature in grades K–4. They may think that some materials are intrinsically warm (blankets or mittens) or cold (metals) (Driver et al. 1994).

- Studies have discovered a vast store of ideas about thermal phenomena in children ages 10–12—for example: heat makes things rise, heat and cold are material substances that can be transferred from one thing to another, and heat accumulates in some areas and flows to others (Erickson 1979, 1980).

- Studies in England found that even though many 14- and 16-year-old students have been exposed to formal instruction about heat, most students still seem to associate the term *heat* with the meanings they have constructed for it during their everyday encounters with hot and cold objects rather than from those encountered in the classroom (Erickson 1985).

- Students gave various responses to researchers to describe the difference between heat and temperature, including (1) there is no difference between them (the most common response), (2) temperature is a measurement of heat, and (3) temperature is the effect of heat (Ericks 1985)

## Suggestions for Instruction and Assessment

- This probe can be followed up as an inquiry-based investigation. Ask the question, encourage students to commit to a prediction, and then test it. The dissonance involved in discovering that the temperature remains the same should be followed with opportunities for students to discuss their ideas and resolve the dissonance. Be aware that in a similar study conducted with elementary students investigating a similar problem by placing thermometers inside a coat, the initial results were not enough to change their thinking. Students believed the thermometer needed to stay inside the coat for a longer period of time. It took successive trials with varying lengths of time before some students (but not all) would accept the idea that the temperature remains the same. Some students will also challenge the results by saying the thermometer is defective.

- Provide a variety of experiences with heat and energy transfer so students can understand the different forms and how they are measured.

- Instruction about heat, temperature, and heat exchange should be carried out over longer periods of time and revisited rather than being taught in just one unit.

- Students may hear and use words like *heat conductor* and *insulator* but may not understand them in the context of a problem such as this probe.

- During elementary years students should have multiple opportunities to identify things that give off heat and things that

do not seem to give off heat in order to develop the idea of a heat source. At this level students can identify obvious heat sources, such as a lightbulb.

- At the middle level, the more abstract idea of "cold" objects as sources of heat can be addressed. For example, challenge students to consider how an ice cube can be considered a source of heat.

- Explicitly address the idea that the heat needed to warm something, such as your hands inside a mitten, must come from somewhere. This leads to discussions that trace where the energy comes from and where it will go and leads students to see how body heat is trapped inside the mitten.

## Related NSTA Science Store Publications and NSTA Journal Articles

Driver, R., A. Squires, P. Rushworth, and V. Wood-Robinson. 1994. *Making sense of secondary science: Research into children's ideas.* London and New York: RoutledgeFalmer.

Keeley, P. 2005. *Science curriculum topic study: Bridging the gap between standards and practice.* Thousand Oaks, CA: Corwin Press.

Robertson, W. 2002. *Energy: Stop faking it! Finally understanding science so you can teach it.* Arlington, VA: NSTA Press.

**Related Curriculum Topic Study Guides**
(Keeley 2005)
"Energy"
"Heat and Temperature"

## References

American Association for the Advancement of Science (AAAS). 1993. *Benchmarks for science literacy.* New York: Oxford University Press.

Driver, R., A. Squires, P. Rushworth, and V. Wood-Robinson. 1994. *Making sense of secondary science: Research into children's ideas.* London and New York: RoutledgeFalmer.

Erickson, G. 1979. Children's conception of heat and temperature. *Science Education* 63: 231–230.

Erickson, G. 1980. Children's viewpoints of heat: A second look. *Science Education* 64: 323–336.

Erickson, G. 1985. Heat and temperature: An overview of children's ideas. In *Children's ideas in science,* eds. R. Driver, E. Guesne, and A. Tiberghien. Milton Keynes, UK: Open University Press.

Keeley, P. 2005. *Science curriculum topic study: Bridging the gap between standards and practice.* Thousand Oaks, CA: Corwin Press.

National Research Council (NRC). 1996. *National science education standards.* Washington, DC: National Academy Press.

# Objects and Temperature

Taz and Kyle are comparing the temperature readings of four different objects:

- block of wood
- metal tray
- wool hat
- glass plate

They place the objects on a table in their science classroom and leave them overnight. A thermometer is attached to each object. The next day they record the temperature of each object at the same time.

Put an X next to the statement that best describes your prediction about the objects' temperature.

_____ None of the objects will have the same temperature.

_____ Two of the objects will have the same temperature.

_____ Three of the objects will have the same temperature.

_____ All of the objects will have the same temperature.

Describe your thinking. Provide an explanation for your answer.

_____

_____

_____

_____

# Objects and Temperature

## Teacher Notes

## Purpose

The purpose of this assessment probe is to elicit students' ideas about temperature. The task specifically probes to find out whether students recognize that non-heat-producing objects exposed to the same ambient conditions will have the same temperature, regardless of the material they are made of.

## Related Concepts

heat, energy, temperature

## Explanation

The best response is that all of the objects will be at the same temperature. Heat is generally a measure of the total kinetic energy of the molecules in a system. Temperature is gener-

ally a measure of the average kinetic energy of the molecules. In this example all the objects are exposed to the same ambient conditions. There is no detectable transfer of energy resulting in additional energy being absorbed or lost by the material that would change the average motion of their atoms or molecules and thus change the temperature. Therefore, since the average motion of the atoms or molecules does not change, the temperature remains the same. What is confusing is that when these objects are touched, some may appear to be "colder" or "warmer" than others. For example, the metal tray feels colder than the wool hat. Energy flows from warmer objects to cooler ones. Your hand at body temperature, which is warmer

than room temperature, will transfer heat to the object touched. An object like metal is a better heat conductor than an object like the wool hat. Therefore, it will conduct heat from your hand faster. As a result, the metal feels cooler to you than the hat. They are at the same temperature, however, because the average kinetic energy of their particles is the same.

## Curricular and Instructional Considerations

### Elementary Students

Students' experiences with materials in their environment may intuitively affect their idea that the temperatures will be different. Any young student who has touched metal on a cold day and touched wood exposed to the same conditions would infer that the metal has a colder temperature. Younger students will also believe some materials appear to be inherently cold, such as metals, or warm, such as hats. Students at this level do not conceptually distinguish between heat and temperature. However, it is a grade-level expectation in the national standards that students will understand that heat moves by conduction. Yet, linking this idea to what happens when you touch different objects and they feel warmer or colder is a more sophisticated idea that develops later in middle school. This probe is useful in determining the intuitive ideas students have about the temperature of everyday objects.

### Middle School Students

Students at this level will continue to confuse heat and temperature and fail to recognize the heat transfer involved when heat-conducting objects are touched. The idea that heat results from the motion of molecules and that a transfer of energy is involved when there is a change in heat is a grade-level expectation in the middle and high school standards. However, this is still an abstract notion. The probe is useful in determining if students still persist in their intuitive notions about heat and temperature.

### High School Students

Heat and temperature ideas become more complex at this age. Yet, students may still hold onto similar ideas they had in elementary grades. High school students build on their experiences with energy transfer in the middle grades to investigate heat quantitatively by measuring variables such as temperature change and kinetic energy (NRC 1996). However, misconceptions about energy transfer and the distinction between heat and temperature may still persist and be uncovered through use of this probe.

### Administering the Probe

Be sure students understand that the objects on the table are all experiencing the same conditions, including the same room temperature. You may wish to model the probe scenario and have students touch the objects before answering the probe or show them the objects to remind them what the materials are. This probe can be combined with "The Mitten Problem" (p. 103) to assess ideas about heat energy and temperature in a different context.

## Related Ideas in *National Science Education Standards* (NRC 1996)

. . . . . . . . . . . . . . . . . . . . . . . . . . . . . . .

### K–4 Light, Heat, Electricity, and Magnetism

- Heat can be produced in many ways, such as burning, rubbing, or mixing one substance with another. Heat can move from one object to another by conduction.

### 5–8 Transfer of Energy

- Energy is a property of many substances and is associated with heat, light, electricity, mechanical motion, sound, nuclei, and the nature of a chemical. Energy is transferred in many ways.
- ★ Heat moves in predictable ways, flowing from warmer objects to cooler ones, until both reach the same temperature.

### 9–12 Conservation of Energy and the Increase in Disorder

- ★ Heat consists of random motion and the vibrations of atoms, molecules, and ions. The higher the temperature, the greater the atomic or molecular motion.

## Related Ideas in *Benchmarks for Science Literacy* (AAAS 1993)

. . . . . . . . . . . . . . . . . . . . . . . . . . . . . .

### 3–5 Energy Transformation

- Heat is produced by mechanical and electrical machines and any time one thing rubs up against another.

- ★ When warmer things are put with cooler ones, the warm ones lose heat and the cool ones gain it until they are all at the same temperature.
- Poor conductors can reduce heat loss.

### 6–8 Energy Transformation

- Energy cannot be created or destroyed, but only changed from one form into another.
- Energy appears in different forms. Heat energy is in the disorderly motion of molecules.

### 9–12 Energy Transformation

- Heat energy in a material consists of the disordered motions of its atoms or molecules.
- Transformations of energy usually produce some energy in the form of heat, which spreads around by radiation or conduction into cooler places.

## Related Research

- Students in the age range of 8–12 are able to use and read a thermometer to take temperature readings. They tend to make judgments about the temperature of an object based more on the nature of the material than the temperature of the surrounding medium (Erickson 1985).
- Students are likely to think that objects of different materials in the same room will be at different temperatures even if they are told that the objects are kept at room temperature (Erickson 1985).
- One place students would be expected

---

★ Indicates a strong match between the ideas elicited by the probe and a national standard's learning goal.

to understand the distinction between heat and temperature is in chemistry classes. However, most of the chemistry problems assigned to students in introductory chemistry classes do not require students to make the distinction, so students have little opportunity to acquire the distinction. Chemistry teachers may be unaware that students lack this skill and may have the expectation that they do understand the difference (Gabel and Bunce 1994).

- The concept of thermal equilibrium when several objects are in prolonged contact with the same air in the same room is often missing. Students have difficulty recognizing the equality of temperatures at thermal equilibrium (Tiberghien 1985).

## Suggestions for Instruction and Assessment

- This probe can be followed up as an inquiry-based investigation. Ask the question, encourage students to commit to a prediction, and then test it. The dissonance involved in discovering that the temperatures are the same should be followed with opportunities for students to discuss their ideas and resolve the dissonance.

- Provide opportunities for students to investigate the temperature of different materials in the same warm and cold surroundings.

- Help students understand what is happening when you touch metal versus when you touch a wool hat or block of wood. Help

them use ideas about conduction and transfer of energy in this context to explain why it feels as if they are at different temperatures.

- Use everyday examples such as why you would rather stand on a rug in your bathroom on a cold morning if you are in your bare feet than stand on the bathroom tiles. Use multiple examples like this to relate the idea that objects may feel warmer or colder even though the temperature is the same.

- Be careful how you use terms such as *heat* and *temperature* and alert students to examples.

- Instruction about heat, temperature, and heat exchange should be carried out over a long period and not in one single instructional unit. These are difficult ideas that take time and multiple experiences to develop.

SCI**LINKS**
*THE WORLD'S A CLICK AWAY*

**Topic: Heat/Temperature**
**Go to:** *www.scilinks.org*
**Code: USIS107**

## Related NSTA Science Store Publications and NSTA Journal Articles

Driver, R., A. Squires, P. Rushworth, and V. Wood-Robinson. 1994. *Making sense of secondary science: Research into children's ideas.* London and New York: RoutledgeFalmer.

Keeley, P. 2005. *Science curriculum topic study: Bridging the gap between standards and practice.* Thousand Oaks, CA: Corwin Press.

Robertson, W. 2002. *Energy: Stop faking it! Finally understanding science so you can teach it.* Arlington, VA: NSTA Press.

**Related Curriculum Topic Study Guide**
(Keeley 2005)
"Heat and Temperature"

## References

American Association for the Advancement of Science (AAAS). 1993. *Benchmarks for science literacy.* New York: Oxford University Press.

Erickson, G. 1985. Heat and temperature: An overview of children's ideas. In *Children's ideas in science,* eds. R. Driver, E. Guesne, and A. Tiberghien. Milton Keynes, UK: Open University Press.

Gabel, D., and D. Bunce. 1994. Research on problem solving in chemistry. In *Handbook of research on science teaching and learning,* ed. D. Gabel. New York: Simon and Schuster.

Keeley, P. 2005. *Science curriculum topic study: Bridging the gap between standards and practice.* Thousand Oaks, CA: Corwin Press.

National Research Council (NRC). 1996. *National science education standards.* Washington, DC: National Academy Press.

Tiberghien, A. 1985. Heat and temperature: The development of ideas with teaching. In *Children's ideas in science,* eds. R. Driver, E. Guesne, and A. Tiberghien. Milton Keynes, UK: Open University Press.

# Life, Earth, and Space Science Assessment Probes

# Probes

| Core Science Concepts | Organisms | | Structure and Function | | | Earth Processes | | | Phases of the Moon | |
|---|---|---|---|---|---|---|---|---|---|---|
| | Is It an Animal? | Is It Living? | Is It Made of Cells? | Human Body Basics | Functions of Living Things | Wet Jeans | Beach Sand | Mountain Age | Gazing at the Moon | Going Through a Phase |
| Animals | ✓ | | | | | | | | | |
| Classification | ✓ | | | | | | | | | |
| Life Processes | | ✓ | | ✓ | ✓ | | | | | |
| Living Things | | ✓ | | | | | | | | |
| Characteristics of Life | | ✓ | | | | | | | | |
| Cells | | | ✓ | ✓ | | | | | | |
| Cellular Processes | | | | ✓ | ✓ | | | | | |
| Levels of Organization in Living Systems | | | | ✓ | | | | | | |
| Structure and Function | | | | ✓ | | | | | | |
| Photosynthesis | | | | | ✓ | | | | | |
| Respiration | | | | | ✓ | | | | | |
| Similarities Within the Diversity of Life | | | | | ✓ | | | | | |
| Water Cycle | | | | | | ✓ | | | | |
| Evaporation | | | | | | ✓ | | | | |
| Weathering | | | | | | | ✓ | ✓ | | |
| Erosion | | | | | | | ✓ | | | |
| Deposition | | | | | | | ✓ | ✓ | | |
| Landforms | | | | | | | | ✓ | | |
| Mountains | | | | | | | | ✓ | | |
| Moon Phases | | | | | | | | | ✓ | ✓ |

# Is It an Animal?

Which of the organisms listed are animals? Put an X next to each organism that is considered to be an animal.

| | |
|---|---|
| ___ cow | ___ spider |
| ___ tree | ___ snail |
| ___ mushroom | ___ flower |
| ___ human | ___ monkey |
| ___ worm | ___ beetle |
| ___ tiger | ___ whale |
| ___ shark | ___ frog | ___ mold |
| ___ starfish | ___ chicken | ___ snake |

Explain your thinking. Describe the "rule" or reasoning you used to decide if something is an animal.

_____

_____

_____

_____

_____

_____

_____

_____

_____

# Is It an Animal?

## Teacher Notes

## Purpose

The purpose of this assessment probe is to elicit students' ideas about animals. The probe specifically seeks to find out what characteristics students use to determine whether an organism is classified as an animal.

## Related Concepts

animals, classification

## Explanation

The cow, human, worm, tiger, shark, starfish, spider, snail, monkey, beetle, whale, frog, chicken, and snake are biologically classified as animals. The tree and flower are classified as plants, and the mushroom and mold are classified as fungi. Biological classification at the kingdom level places more emphasis on

cellular details (including molecular details), anatomical details (internal and external structures), and embryology than on general appearance or behavior. Animals have body plans and internal structures that enable them to obtain their food from an external source, making them consumers (or heterotrophs). All animals are consumers; however, not all consumers are animals. Animals are multicellular and their cells do not contain cell walls. Their embryonic development starts with a diploid zygote (product of the union of egg and sperm), and a defining characteristic of all animals that differentiates them from other heterotrophs is that they develop from a blastula (this is a complex idea that isn't developed until later in high school or college). The animal kingdom contains a vast variety of life forms,

including diverse examples from phyla such as sponges, coelenterates (e.g., jellyfish), mollusks (e.g., snails), worms, arthropods (e.g., insects), echinoderms (e.g., starfish), and vertebrates (including the classes of fish, amphibians, reptiles, birds, and mammals).

## Curricular and Instructional Considerations

### Elementary Students

By the time children enter school they are quite familiar with animals (from barnyards, backyards, and zoos and as pets) and have begun to form an operative definition for whether or not something is considered to be an animal. Their ideas are quite concrete and they tend to associate animals with pets or animals kept in a zoo, based on their everyday experiences. Their instruction focuses on a variety of animals and their needs and characteristics. However, students' learning may become quite limited if they focus only on familiar animals, particularly mammals or other vertebrates. This probe is useful in determining what characteristics students initially use to help them decide if a living organism is an animal, based on their familiarity with a variety of animals.

### Middle School

In middle school, students begin to develop formal distinctions between plants and animals based on whether plants and animals make their own food and on their internal structures. Animals are considered consumers, but students may fail to recognize that a vari-

ety of different types of consumers are also animals. This idea is a grade-level expectation in the national standards. Biological diversity is addressed; however, students may still have a limited view of what an animal is.

SCI LINKS.
THE WORLD'S A CLICK AWAY

**Topic: Classification**
**Go to:** *www.scilinks.org*
**Code: USIS119**

### High School

Students at this level exhibit a general understanding of taxonomic classification and use hierarchical groupings to understand that seemingly different organisms in different phyla belong to the animal kingdom. This probe is useful in determining whether students revert to their own operative definitions of an animal, even after formal biological instruction in middle or high school.

### Administering the Probe

Eliminate any organisms that students are not familiar with. Elementary teachers may want to include pictures with each example. In lower elementary grades, it is helpful to have students complete the top part of the task on their own, followed by individual student interviews or a group discussion, enabling the teacher to more fully capture students' thinking. Teachers may also wish to tailor the list of items to better fit their teaching context. Middle and high school teachers may want to add organisms from all the kingdoms of life. This probe also works well in a group situation, having students vote on whether or not they think an organism is an animal and then discuss their reasons with the class. This probe can also be

used as a card sort. Ask students to work in small groups or pairs to sort cards of the names and/or pictures of organisms into two groups: those that are considered to be animals and those that are not. Observe and listen to students discuss their reasons with their peers as they sort the cards.

## Related Ideas in *National Science Education Standards* (NRC 1996)

· · · · · · · · · · · · · · · · · · · · · · · · · · · · ·

### K–4 The Characteristics of Organisms

- Each plant or animal has different structures that serve different functions in growth, survival, and reproduction. For example, humans have distinct body structures for walking, holding, seeing, and talking.

### 5–8 Diversity and Adaptations of Organisms

- ★ Millions of species of animals, plants, and microorganisms are alive today. Although different species might look dissimilar, the unity among organisms becomes apparent from an analysis of internal structures, the similarity of their chemical processes, and the evidence of common ancestry.

### 9–12 Biological Evolution

- Biological classifications are based on how organisms are related. Organisms are classified into a hierarchy of groups and subgroups based on similarities that reflect their evolutionary relationships.

## Related Ideas in *Benchmarks for Science Literacy* (AAAS 1993)

· · · · · · · · · · · · · · · · · · · · · · · · · · · · ·

### K–2 Diversity of Life

- Some animals (and plants) are alike in the way they look and in the things they do, and others are very different from one another.

### 3–5 Diversity of Life

- ★ A great variety of kinds of living things can be sorted into groups in many ways using various features to decide which things belong to which group.

### 6–8 Diversity of Life

- ★ One of the most general distinctions among organisms is between plants, which use sunlight to make their own food, and animals, which consume energy-rich foods. Some kinds of organisms, many of them microscopic, cannot be neatly classified as either plants or animals.

## Related Research

- People of all ages have a much narrower definition of an animal than biologists. Typically, students think of "animals" as large, terrestrial mammals. Animal qualities commonly include the following: having four legs, being large in size, having fur, making noise, and living on land. A study of 15-year-olds found that 10% identified animals as a biologist would from an assortment of organisms. About half of these

---

★ Indicates a strong match between the ideas elicited by the probe and a national standard's learning goal.

students identified fish, boy, frog, snail, snake, and whale as animals (Bell 1981).

- Older students often apply more general characteristics that apply to all living things (i.e., respiration and reproducing) to animals (Trowbridge and Mintzes 1985).

- Some students, although they recognize feeding as an attribute, see it as a general characteristic of living things rather than in terms of the heterotrophic nature of the way animals feed (Driver et al. 1994).

- Studies show that preservice elementary teachers, as well as experienced elementary teachers, also hold restricted meanings for the concept of "animal" (Driver et al. 1994). This may affect students' opportunities to learn the scientific view of "animal."

- Humans are often not thought of as animals; rather they are contrasted with animals. Humans, insects, birds, and fish are often thought of as alternatives other than animals, not as subsets of animals (Driver et al. 1994).

## Suggestions for Instruction and Assessment

- National standards suggest the study of living organisms begin with those that are most familiar to younger students—those found in their immediate environment. Be careful that this does not limit the child's experience to only vertebrates, particularly mammals. In later years, have students study a variety of animals representing the diversity of animal life.

- When students group organisms as ani-

mals, it is important that instruction is geared toward getting students to carefully examine the characteristics to see if they are truly exclusive.

- Instruction related to animals is often focused on a specific organism or organisms (e.g., butterflies or barnyard animals). This may help students develop an understanding of the special characteristics of butterflies or barnyard animals that define them as animals, but students may fail to generalize to other vertebrate and invertebrate classes.

- Encourage students to examine animals carefully. Identify attributes in common, even though the animals may appear to be very different.

- Provide multiple experiences in sorting and classifying animals, emphasizing the characteristics that are consistent with a particular grouping. Introduce students to the hierarchical nature of groupings (e.g., A robin is both a bird and an animal.)

- Explicitly develop the idea that all animals are consumers, but make sure that older students understand that not all consumers are animals (e.g., protists). Use nutrition as the initial way to distinguish animals from plants.

- Help students understand that the way we use words in everyday life may be different from the way words are used in science. Remind them that the word *animal* has a much more precise meaning in science than in everyday language. Be aware that the more commonly used a word is in everyday language, such as *animal*, the more likely students are to revert back to a lay

definition. Once students develop a formal definition of *animal*, challenge them to think of everyday usages of the word that would be limiting. For example, if a sign outside a store says, "No animals allowed," would you be allowed to enter the store?

- Use the interview protocol developed by Charles Barman (Barman et al. 1999) to further examine students' ideas about animals. Combine this with several other types of ways to categorize animals versus non-animals.

- Be aware that accepting humans as animals may be more than a shift in scientific thinking. Some students may have cultural or religious traditions that may make them resistant to considering humans as animals. Teachers can respect these beliefs by balancing the scientific notion that humans are biologically classified in the animal kingdom with the notion that humans are a unique and very special kind of animal.

## Related NSTA Science Store Publications and NSTA Journal Articles

Barman, C., N. Barman, K. Berglund, and M. Goldston. 1999. Assessing students' ideas about animals. *Science and Children* (Sept.): 44–49.

Driver, R., A. Squires, P. Rushworth, and V. Wood-Robinson. 1994. *Making sense of secondary science: Research into children's ideas.* London and New York: RoutledgeFalmer.

Keeley, P. 2005. *Science curriculum topic study: Bridging the gap between standards and practice.*

Thousand Oaks, CA: Corwin Press.

Stovall, G., and C. Nesbit. 2003. Let's try action research. *Science and Children* (Feb.): 44–48.

### Related Curriculum Topic Study Guides
(Keeley 2005)
"Animal Life"
"Biological Classification"
"Biodiversity"

## References

American Association for the Advancement of Science (AAAS). 1993. *Benchmarks for science literacy.* New York: Oxford University Press.

Barman, C., N. Barman, K. Berglund, and M. Goldston. 1999. Assessing students' ideas about animals. *Science and Children* (Sept.): 44–49.

Bell, B. 1981. When is an animal not an animal? *Journal of Biological Education* 15 (3): 213–218.

Driver, R., A. Squires, P. Rushworth, and V. Wood-Robinson. 1994. *Making sense of secondary science: Research into children's ideas.* London and New York: RoutledgeFalmer.

Keeley, P. 2005. *Science curriculum topic study: Bridging the gap between standards and practice.* Thousand Oaks, CA: Corwin Press.

National Research Council (NRC). 1996. *National science education standards.* Washington, DC: National Academy Press.

Trowbridge, J., and J. Mintzes. 1985. Students' alternative conceptions of animal classification. *School Science and Mathematics* 85 (4): 304–316.

# Is It Living?

Listed below are examples of living (which includes once-living) and nonliving things. Put an X next to the things that could be considered living.

_____ tree        _____ egg

_____ rock        _____ bacteria

_____ fire        _____ cell

_____ boy         _____ molecule

_____ wind        _____ Sun

_____ rabbit      _____ mushroom

_____ cloud       _____ potato

_____ feather     _____ leaf

_____ grass       _____ butterfly        _____ fossil            _____ mitochondria

_____ seed        _____ pupae            _____ hibernating bear  _____ river

Explain your thinking. What "rule" or reasoning did you use to decide if something could be considered living?

_____

_____

_____

_____

_____

_____

_____

_____

_____

# Is It Living?

## Teacher Notes

### Purpose

The purpose of this assessment probe is to elicit students' ideas about living and nonliving things. The probe is designed to find out what attributes children focus on when considering if something is or was once living.

### Related Concepts

living things, life processes, characteristics of life

### Explanation

Differentiating between living and nonliving is not a simple black-and-white task. There is no single criterion used to identify whether something is living. Additionally, some of the characteristics that are used to identify living things are not easily observable, such as extracting energy from food as opposed to being able to watch an organism "eat." Living things are made up of one or more cells and carry out basic life processes (e.g., acquire or make food, grow, respire, reproduce, react to stimuli, move, and eliminate waste). Not all living things show all of these characteristics all of the time. The tree, boy, rabbit, grass, seed, egg, bacteria, cell, mushroom, potato, leaf, butterfly, pupae, and hibernating bear can be considered living. Each is made up of one or more cells and is capable of performing one or more life processes. The tree, boy, rabbit, grass, bacteria, mushroom, butterfly, and hibernating bear are also complete living organisms. Some of the items listed are living organisms in various developmental stages of their life cycle such as the seed, egg (recognize that an egg from the supermarket is "once living"), and pupae. The potato and leaf are parts of a living plant. By themselves they are capable of carrying out some life processes for a limited time.

The remaining items—cloud, fire, wind, Sun, feather, molecule, river, mitochondria, rock, and fossil—are nonliving. The feather was once part of a living thing, partially made up of cells as well as materials made by cells. However, by itself, it cannot sustain life. The mitochondria are parts of a cell that carry out the process of releasing energy from food but by themselves they are not living. Some things can be living without being a complete organism. For example, a leaf is a part of a complete plant. With a source of water and air, some leaf cuttings can continue to carry out life processes, develop roots, and eventually become an entire plant.

## Curricular and Instructional Considerations

. . . . . . . . . . . . . . . . . . . . . . . . . . . . . .

### Elementary Students

Young children develop their ideas about living organisms based on their conception of living versus nonliving. Students in early elementary grades develop an understanding that living things have basic needs such as food, water, and air. As they progress through the elementary grades, students develop an understanding of several basic observable functions performed by living things such as eating, drinking, breathing, growing, and moving. At this level students are more likely to think of a whole organism as living rather than a part of an organism such as a leaf or cell. This probe is useful in identifying early ideas students have about the concept of living.

### Middle School Students

As students investigate more unfamiliar life forms, they refine their early ideas about living. They begin to develop a more sophisticated understanding of the needs of cells and the life processes occurring at the cellular level—for example, extracting energy from food, removing waste products, taking in water, and cells dividing to make more cells. They also recognize that some living things perform their life functions as a single cell.

Topic: Characteristics of Living Things
Go to: *www.scilinks.org*
Code: USIS125

### High School Students

By high school, students have a more complete understanding of the processes that support life, particularly at the cellular level. They have a greater ability to recognize the ubiquitous features and processes common to all life from the early stages of development to adult. They recognize death as the cessation of life processes. This probe is useful in comparing high school students' conception of living with elementary and middle school students' ideas and determining whether the high schoolers have accumulated the biological ideas that can be used to explain life and death.

### Administering the Probe

During the administration of this task, consider interviewing students and/or using props. Tailor the items on this list to suit targeted instructional goals and the developmental levels of students. Remove items that are unfamiliar. Consider including additional items for

younger students, such as tadpoles, a cocoon or butterfly chrysalis, bulbs, and a plant cutting. For older students consider adding items like bread mold, yeast, a virus, DNA and proteins, additional parts of a cell, and/or a fresh bone. This task can also be used as a card sort. Provide students with cards printed with various examples and ask them to work with a partner or small group to sort them into piles of "living" and "nonliving." Listen carefully to their explanations as they sort.

## Related Ideas in *National Science Education Standards* (NRC 1996)

### K–4 Characteristics of Organisms

*   Organisms have basic needs. For example, animals need air, water, and food; plants require air, water, nutrients, and light.

### 5–8 Structure and Function in Living Systems

*   All organisms are composed of cells, the fundamental units of life.

### 9–12 Matter, Energy, and Organization in Living Systems

*   Living systems require a continuous input of energy to maintain their chemical and physical organizations. With death, and the cessation of energy input, living systems rapidly disintegrate.
*   The complexity and organization of organisms accommodate the need for obtaining, transforming, transporting, releasing, and eliminating the matter and energy used to sustain the organism.

## Related Ideas in *Benchmarks for Science Literacy* (AAAS 1993)

### K–2 Cells

*   Most living things need water, food, and air.

### 3–5 Cells

*   Some living things consist of a single cell. Like familiar organisms, they need food, water, and air; a way to dispose of waste; and an environment they can live in.

### 6–8 Cells

*   All living things are composed of cells, from just one to many millions, whose details usually are visible only through a microscope.

## Related Research

*   Children have various ideas about what constitutes living. Some may believe objects that are "active" are alive—for example, fire, clouds, or the Sun. As children mature they include eating, breathing, and reproducing as essential characteristics of living things. People of all ages use movement, and in particular movement as a response to a stimulus, as a defining characteristic of life. When doing so, these individuals tend to omit plants from the living category. Some studies show that young

children will infrequently give "growth" as a criterion for life, the exception being when plants are identified as living—then "growth" is commonly given as the reason (Driver et al. 1994).

- A study by Stavy and Wax (1989) revealed that children seem to have different views for "animal life" and "plant life." In general, animals were more often recognized as being alive than plants.

- Some studies indicate that the ability to reproduce is occasionally given by young children as a criterion for life. However, some nonliving things were said to be living because they "reproduced" (Driver et al. 1994).

- Elementary and middle school students use observable processes such as movement, breathing, reproducing, and dying when deciding if things are alive or not. High school and college students use these same readily observable characteristics to determine if something is alive. They rarely mention ideas such as "being made up of cells" or biochemical aspects such as "containing DNA." It has been suggested that the learning of facts has contributed little toward understanding. Students may be able to quote the seven characteristics of life but may not be able to apply them when determining if something is living (Brumby 1982).

- In a study of 424 Israeli students ages 8–14, Tamir, Gal-Chappin, and Nussnovitz (1981) found no significant difference in age when students were asked to classify 16

pictures as living or nonliving things. On average, 20% of the items were grouped incorrectly, with trees, mushrooms, Sun, rivers, embryos, eggs, and seeds being problematic.

- Objects that children anthropomorphized are categorized as living things. For example, objects such as the Sun, cars, wind, and fire "felt" and "knew" things and were therefore alive. Studies indicate that there is a marked shift as students age from the view that objects and things (including living things) carry out certain tasks "because they want to" to reasoning that "they need to in order to live" (Driver et al. 1994).

- Carey (1985) suggested that progression in the concept of "living" is linked to growth in children's ideas about biological processes. Young children have little knowledge of biology. In addition, it isn't until around the age of 9–10 years that children begin to understand death as the cessation of life processes.

- Some of the earliest studies on children's conception of living were carried out by Piaget. His results showed a predictable pattern in students' development of the concept "living." From ages 0 to 5, students have almost no concept for living things; from ages 6 to 7 students believe things that are active or make noise are alive; from ages 8 to 9 students classify things that move as alive; from ages 9 to 11 students place things that appear to move by themselves (including rivers and the Sun) as living; and over age 11 through

adulthood animals or animals and plants are considered living (Driver et al. 1994).

## Suggestions for Instruction and Assessment

- Engage students in thought-provoking exercises that allow them to "discover" why things are considered to be alive. Have students monitor and observe a number of items that are classified as "living"—from whole organisms to parts of organisms such as a carrot top placed in a dish of water. Have them generate their own characteristics of what makes these things "alive." Include items that may not be readily classified as "alive," such as plant seeds, flower bulbs, potatoes, mushrooms, and insect pupae.

- Give students an unusual object (e.g., strange-looking rock, dried piece of sponge, brine shrimp eggs, fossil, green "slime") and tell them it was found in an isolated area such as a remote rain forest. Challenge them to come up with ways to find out if it is alive, dead but once living, or never alive. Have them present their evidence to support their ideas.

- Place emphasis on the "living" aspects when studying life cycles and show that death is the end of the life cycle for an individual organism. Students often think that organisms in metamorphic or dormant states are dead. Counteract this with what happens after they emerge from such states and with the idea that they had to be alive for their life cycles to continue.

- Emphasis in the early grades should be placed on familiar animals (including people) and plants and progressing to more complex or unusual organisms (e.g., single celled) in later grades. Students should be encouraged to look for similarities when considering the needs and functions of living things.

- Beginning around third grade, students' observations of living things should include microscopic organisms. Students should be given the opportunity to make the connection that microscopic life has basic characteristics similar to more familiar, larger organisms. For example, they use the same things (e.g., food, water) and carry out similar processes that will keep them alive.

- Be sure to distinguish needs from processes. For example, a seed may not need water for many years while it is dormant, but once environmental conditions are right and it can take in water it will grow into a plant capable of sustaining life. Lessons should address the many life processes as students progress through the grades—use of food for energy, reproduction, reaction to stimuli, transport of materials, gas exchange, movement, waste elimination, and so forth.

- Be aware of the tendency of younger children to anthropomorphize. Explore the use of common phrases that imply nonliving things do the same things as living things—for example, a fire "breathes" or waves "grow." Pay close attention to lit-

erature and images that make nonliving things seem living, such as putting a face on the Sun or clouds.

- Have young students compare and contrast a stuffed animal toy with the real thing. Ask questions such as, What can the living animal do that the stuffed toy cannot do? Why is one considered living and the other not? Is the stuffed animal toy dead or was it never alive? How do you know?

- Use the mnemonic, MRS GREN, to help students identify the seven life processes that characterize life: M = movement, R = respiration, S = stimuli (reaction to), G = growth, R = reproduction, E = elimination of wastes, and N = nutrition (acquiring of or making food). Make sure students know what these processes mean and that not all living things will show all of them all of the time.

- In middle and high school, make sure students understand the cell as the basic unit of function that carries out the life processes. The idea that all living things are composed of cells (assuming viruses are nonliving) is the most fundamental way to define *living* or *once living*.

## Related NSTA Science Store Publications and NSTA Journal Articles

Aram, R., and B. Bradshaw. 2001. How do children know what they know? *Science and Children* (Oct.): 28–33.

Driver, R., A. Squires, P. Rushworth, and V. Wood-Robinson. 1994. *Making sense of secondary sci-*

ence: Research into children's ideas. London and New York: RoutledgeFalmer.

Keeley, P. 2005. *Science curriculum topic study: Bridging the gap between standards and practice.* Thousand Oaks, CA: Corwin Press.

**Related Curriculum Topic Study Guides**
(Keeley 2005)
"Characteristics of Living Things"
"Life Processes and the Needs of Organisms"

## References

American Association for the Advancement of Science (AAAS). 1993. *Benchmarks for science literacy.* New York: Oxford University Press.

Brumby, M. 1982. Students' perceptions of the concept of life. *Science Education* 66 (4): 613–622.

Carey, S. 1985. *Conceptual change in childhood.* Cambridge, MA: MIT Press.

Driver, R., A. Squires, P. Rushworth, and V. Wood-Robinson. 1994. *Making sense of secondary science: Research into children's ideas.* London and New York: RoutledgeFalmer.

Keeley, P. 2005. *Science curriculum topic study: Bridging the gap between standards and practice.* Thousand Oaks, CA: Corwin Press.

National Research Council (NRC). 1996. *National science education standards.* Washington, DC: National Academy Press.

Stavy, R., and N. Wax. 1989. Children's conception of plants as living things. *Human Development* 32: 88–89.

Tamir, P., R. Gal-Chappin, and R. Nussnovitz. 1981. How do intermediate and junior high students conceptualize living and non-living? *Journal of Research in Science Teaching* 18 (3): 241–248.

# Is It Made of Cells?

Imagine you could examine the objects and materials listed below with a powerful microscope. This powerful microscope will allow you to see evidence of cell structure.

Put an X next to the objects or materials that are made up, or were once made up, of cells.

___flowers     ___apples

___skin     ___sand

___proteins     ___worms

___rocks     ___bacteria

___milk     ___leaf

___bone     ___seeds

___lungs     ___water     ___paramecium

___hamburger     ___molecules     ___blood     ___chromosomes

___DNA     ___sugar     ___cell membrane     ___saliva

___calcium     ___chlorophyll     ___mushrooms     ___atoms

Explain your thinking. Describe the "rule" or reason you used to decide whether something is or was once made up of cells.

_____

_____

_____

_____

_____

_____

# Is It Made of Cells?

## Teacher Notes

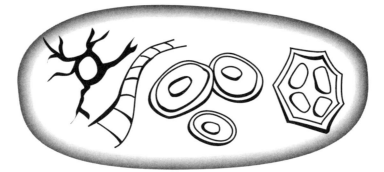

### Purpose

The purpose of this assessment probe is to elicit students' ideas about objects and materials that are made up of cells. The probe is designed to find out how students decide whether something is or was once made up of cells by providing a variety of examples, including living and once-living things, materials that are manufactured by cells but are not composed of cells, parts of a cell, inorganic substances that did not originate from cells, and building blocks of all matter.

### Related Concept

cells

### Explanation

The cell is the fundamental unit of life. Living or once-living things are made up of one or more cells as well as materials made by cells and inorganic materials, such as water, that are found within cells. The materials and objects listed in the probe that are made up of cells are the following: flowers, skin, bone, lungs, hamburger, apples, leaf, worms, bacteria, seeds, paramecium, blood, and mushrooms. All of these materials arose from living cells and are cellular in origin, although they may include noncellular materials (e.g., blood contains plasma as well as blood cells). Some materials, such as milk and saliva, are made by cells and are found outside of cells, but are not cellular in structure. They are products of cells and do not give rise to new cells. Materials found inside a cell include molecules such as DNA, sugar, chlorophyll, and proteins as well as elements like calcium that give bone tissue its strength. Objects that are organelles, parts of a cell, include the cell membrane and chromosomes. The remaining items—rocks, water, and sand—are not made up of cells but are made up of matter. Molecules and atoms

are the basic building blocks of cells as well as all matter. Cells use, manufacture, or contain/transform several of the noncellular materials that are commonly associated with cells, such as sugars and proteins, but these materials are not cellular in structure.

## Curricular and Instructional Considerations

### Elementary Students

Upper elementary students are just beginning to learn about cells as the basic unit of structure. Experiences include looking at cells in tissues of familiar plants and animals as well as single-celled organisms. Items on the list should be limited to those that students are familiar with. This probe is useful in finding out if students have beginning ideas that all living or once-living organisms and parts of organisms are made of cells. It may be useful to combine this probe with "Is It Living?" (p. 123).

### Middle School Students

Middle school students expand their developing knowledge about cells to include materials made by cells and materials that are inside of cells. They also recognize that structures such as tissues and organs are part of a hierarchy that is traced back to the cell. They may begin developing additional hierarchies that include cell structures as well as molecules found inside of cells. The challenge with middle school students is in helping them overcome the idea that living things do not contain cells but rath-

er that living things are cellular. Knowing that anything living is made up of cells, which would include most parts of an organism, is a grade-level expectation in the national standards. In middle school, students are also developing ideas about fundamental units of matter such as atoms and molecules. Often these ideas are taught separately and students may confuse the two when the context changes. This probe is useful in probing beyond the idea that the cell is the basic unit of living material and finding out if students can apply this idea to determine if various materials are or were once cellular.

Topic: Cells
Go to: *www.scilinks.org*
Code: USIS133

### High School Students

Students' understanding of cells has expanded to include intracellular structures, biomolecules within the cell, and materials produced and secreted by cells. Ideas in chemistry and biology converge so that students begin to understand that atoms and molecules make up living matter, including cells, as well as nonliving matter. This probe is useful in determining if students prior to and after biological instruction have an understanding of what determines whether materials are made of cells as well as an understanding of the hierarchical nature of cellular composition, including atoms, molecules, and organelles found within the cell.

### Administering the Probe

Limit the items to materials with which students have had direct experience or those with which students have some familiarity. Even though

items on the list such as atoms and molecules are beyond the scope of elementary instruction, it may be interesting to find out students' initial conceptions as they are words young students encounter frequently in the media but have limited conceptions of. Knowing how students formulate ideas early on may provide useful information at the middle level and above.

This probe may be used as a card sort. Have students work in pairs or small groups to discuss and sort the cards into two piles: made of cells and not made of cells. Listen carefully to students' ideas as they discuss their reasons. The probe "Is It Made of Molecules?" (p. 85) may be used along with this probe to determine if middle and high school students confuse the concepts of "cell" and "molecule."

## Related Ideas in *National Science Education Standards* (NRC 1996)

· · · · · · · · · · · · · · · · · · · · · · · · · · · ·

### 5–8 Structure and Function in Living Systems

* Important levels of organization for structure and function include cells, organs, tissues, organ systems, whole organisms, and ecosystems.
* ★ All organisms are composed of cells, the fundamental units of life. Most organisms are singlecells; other organisms, including humans, are multicellular.
* Specialized cells perform specialized functions in multicellular organisms. Groups of specialized cells cooperate to form a tissue, such as a muscle. Different tissues

are in turn grouped together to form larger functional units, called organs.

### 5–8 Reproduction and Heredity

* Hereditary information is contained in genes, located in the chromosomes of each cell.

### 9–12 The Cell

* Cells have particular structures that underlie their functions. Every cell is surrounded by a membrane that separates it from the outside world. Inside the cell is a concentrated mixture of thousands of different molecules that form a variety of specialized structures.
* Cells store and use information to guide their functions. The genetic information stored in DNA is used to direct the synthesis of the thousands of proteins each cell requires.
* Plant cells contain chloroplasts, the site of photosynthesis.
* Most of the cells in a human contain two copies of each of 22 different chromosomes.

## Related Ideas in *Benchmarks for Science Literacy* (AAAS 1993)

· · · · · · · · · · · · · · · · · · · · · · · · · · · ·

### 3–5 Cells

* Some living things consist of a single cell.
* ★ Microscopes make it possible to see that living things are mostly made up of cells. Some organisms are made of a collection of similar cells that benefit from cooperating.

---

★ Indicates a strong match between the ideas elicited by the probe and a national standard's learning goal.

### 6–8 Cells

★ All living things are composed of cells, from just one to many millions, whose details usually are visible only through a microscope. Different body tissues and organs are made up of different kinds of cells.

### 9–12 Cells

- Every cell is covered by a membrane that controls what can enter and leave the cell.

- Within every cell are specialized parts for the transport of materials.

- The work of the cell is carried out by the many different types of molecules it assembles, mostly proteins.

- The genetic information encoded in DNA molecules provides instructions for assembling protein molecules.

## Related Research

- Student may have the notion that organisms "contain" cells as opposed to being "made up of" cells (Driver et al. 1994). In other words, students may believe a living organism is like a "sack" filled with cells rather than being composed of a collection of cells.

- Research conducted by Arnold (1983) indicated that students have difficulty differentiating between the concepts of "cell" and "molecule." There is a tendency for students to over-apply the idea that cells are smaller components of *living* things. Students identified any materials encountered in a biology class (carbohydrates, proteins, and water) as being made up of smaller parts called cells. Arnold coined the term *molecell* to describe this notion of organic molecules being considered as cells.

- Many students think that only certain parts of the human body and other living organisms are made up of cells (Driver et al. 1992).

- Dreyfus and Jungwirth (1988, 1989) reported that students confuse orders of magnitude with levels of organization in living systems. Responses from several 16-year-old Israeli students in the study suggest that students think that biomolecules, such as proteins, are bigger than the size of a cell and that single-celled organisms contain miniature replicas of organs like intestines and lungs. Even though students had learned about cells the year before, their knowledge was superficial. Over a third of the students had alternative conceptions about cells.

## Suggestions for Instruction and Assessment

- Issues of size and scale should be addressed when teaching students about cells. Additionally, ideas about materials should be combined with the notion of scale. Students need to understand that cells, like other types of matter, are made up of materials. These materials contain substances that are made up of atoms and molecules. Even though cells are very small and need to be observed with a microscope, help students understand that there are even smaller parts within the cell that are too small to be seen with a microscope.

- As students engage in activities that involve observing cells, encourage precision with the language used to describe cell observations. Reinforce the idea that single-celled organisms are cells and that multicelled organisms are composed of cells. Students may misinterpret a well-intended statement that multicellular organisms are "collections of cells," believing that these organisms somehow contain or hold cells rather than being structurally built out of cells. With older students the idea that an organism is structurally made of cells, rather than a "sack" filled with cells, can be addressed when students examine the idea of an organism arising from a single cell and repeated cell divisions.

- By the end of middle school, cell observations should be widely varied. Include cells from a number of different life forms and their different body parts—plants, animals, fungi, protists, and monera. Students will begin to discover that cells, regardless of what living thing or body part they come from, look remarkably similar. At the same time, students will also recognize that cells have different parts, depending on the type of organism.

- Explicitly address hierarchical issues by having students engage in activities that focus them at various levels, then "zoom in" to a more detailed level and/or "zoom out" to a larger level so that students can get a sense of parts-and-wholes relationships.

- Present cell ideas in a number of contexts to help students understand that cells are a type of matter that contains substances, molecules, and atoms. When students investigate matter in physical science, include examples of living materials. Be aware that when students first learn about atoms, they may also be learning about parts of a cell at the same grade level. Students may be confused by a term like *nucleus* if instruction does not address the differences between the nucleus of an atom and the nucleus of a cell.

## Related NSTA Science Store Publications and NSTA Journal Articles

American Association for the Advancement of Science (AAAS). 2001. *Atlas of science literacy.* (See "Cells and Organs," pp. 74–75.) New York: Oxford University Press.

Driver, R., A. Squires, P. Rushworth, and V. Wood-Robinson. 1994. *Making sense of secondary science: Research into children's ideas.* London and New York: RoutledgeFalmer.

Keeley, P. 2005. *Science curriculum topic study: Bridging the gap between standards and practice.* Thousand Oaks, CA: Corwin Press.

### Related Curriculum Topic Study Guides
(Keeley 2005)
"Cells"
"Chemistry of Life"

## References

American Association for the Advancement of Sci-

ence (AAAS). 1993. *Benchmarks for science literacy.* New York: Oxford University Press.

Arnold, B. 1983. Beware the molecell! *Biology Newsletter* (Aberdeen College of Education) 42: 2–6.

Dreyfus, A., and E. Jungwirth. 1988. The cell concept of tenth graders: Curricular expectations and reality. *International Journal of Science Education* 10 (2): 221–229.

Dreyfus, A., and E. Jungwirth. 1989. The pupil and the living cell: A taxonomy of dysfunctional ideas about an abstract idea. *Journal of Biological Education* 23 (1): 49–55.

Driver, R. et al. 1992. *Life and living processes: Leeds national curriculum support project, Part 2.* Leeds, UK: Leeds City Council and the University of Leeds.

Driver, R., A. Squires, P. Rushworth, and V. Wood-Robinson. 1994. *Making sense of secondary science: Research into children's ideas.* London and New York: RoutledgeFalmer.

Keeley, P. 2005. *Science curriculum topic study: Bridging the gap between standards and practice.* Thousand Oaks, CA: Corwin Press.

National Research Council (NRC). 1996. *National science education standards.* Washington, DC: National Academy Press.

# Human Body Basics

Four students are working on a human body project for their science class. They cannot agree on the basic unit of structure and function in the human body where basic life processes are carried out. These basic processes are getting energy from food, removal of waste molecules, response to stimuli, movement, reproduction, growth, and repair. They debated their ideas as follows:

Paul's argument: Tissues are the basic unit of structure and organs are the basic unit of function.

Tia's argument: Cells are the basic unit of structure and organs are the basic unit of function.

Margy's argument: Cells are the basic unit of structure and function.

Rae's argument: Organs are the basic unit of structure and function.

Which student do you agree with? Describe your thinking. Provide an explanation for your answer.

_____

_____

_____

_____

_____

_____

_____

_____

# Human Body Basics

## Teacher Notes

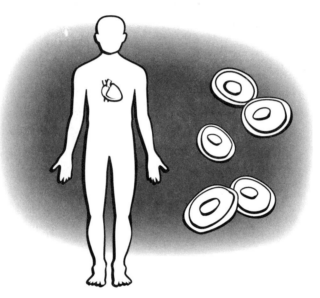

### Purpose

The purpose of this assessment probe is to elicit students' ideas about levels of organization in living organisms. The probe is designed to determine whether students recognize cells as the basic unit of both structure and function for carrying out basic life processes.

### Related Concepts

levels of organization in living systems, cells, structure, function, life processes

### Explanation

Margy's argument is the best answer, although other responses are partially correct. All living things are made of cells. The cell is the basic unit of structure in all living organisms. What is less obvious is that the cell is also the basic unit of function. It is within the cell that most of life's basic processes—such as respiration, eliminating waste molecules, growth, repair, movement, and response—occur. It is within the cell that the complex chemical reactions needed to sustain life occur. This work is carried out by the various molecules within a cell, particularly proteins. In addition to the basic cellular functions common to all cells, specialized cells in multicellular organisms perform functions that support life processes. For example, hormones that regulate body functions are secreted by gland cells, muscle cells contract to support movement of an organism, and nerve cells conduct electrical signals to allow organisms to respond to stimuli. Specialized cells may be arranged as a collection to form tissues, such as muscle, nerve tissue, and blood tissue. The cells within tissues may also be organized to form organs with a specialized purpose such as the brain, heart, and lungs. The human body is a complex multicellular system of cells. Most of the cells in the human body are grouped into organ systems that serve a specific purpose. The organs in these systems depend on cellular processes to carry out essential functions for the organism. It is at the cellular level that molecules are taken in, processed, and transformed, and the resulting products are used directly or distributed elsewhere by interactions among the various systems of the human body.

## Curricular and Instructional Considerations

. . . . . . . . . . . . . . . . . . . . . . . . . . . . .

### Elementary Students

Elementary students develop the idea that organisms, including humans, have various structures that serve different functions. Students begin to make the link between structure and function at the macroscopic level of organs and body systems. They recognize that all living things have to meet the same basic needs in order to survive but do not yet understand these needs are met by the functions of cells. Instruction is primarily focused on external body parts and major organs.

### Middle School Students

Middle school is the time when students are most interested in learning about the human body. At this level students learn about the

various systems and the organs that work together in and across body systems. They develop an understanding that the cell is the fundamental unit of life and that there is a hierarchical organization to the human body. They also begin to develop ideas about basic processes that occur in cells, without an emphasis on the parts of a cell. These are grade-level expectations in the national standards. This probe is useful in determining whether students have a "macro" view of structure and function primarily focused on tissues and/or organs, or if they accept the idea that the cell is both the fundamental unit of structure and function.

**Topic: The Chemistry of Life**
Go to: *www.scilinks.org*
**Code: USIS141**

### High School Students

At this level structure and function is emphasized at the cellular, organelle, and molecular level. This probe is useful in finding out students' ideas before instruction on the cellular, intracellular, and biochemical nature of structure and function as well as determining whether students are able to transfer the cell ideas learned in biology to the context of a human organism.

### Administering the Probe

Be sure to encourage students to explain their thinking. Ask them to provide the reasons why they chose a particular student's point of view.

## Related Ideas in *National Science Education Standards* (NRC 1996)

. . . . . . . . . . . . . . . . . . . . . . . . . . . . .

### K–4 The Characteristics of Organisms

- Each plant or animal has different structures that serve different functions in growth, survival, and reproduction. For example, humans have distinct body structures for walking, holding, seeing, and talking.

### 5–8 Structure and Function in Living Systems

- Living systems at all levels of organization demonstrate the complementary nature of structure and function. Important levels of organization for structure and function include cells, organs, tissues, organ systems, whole organisms, and ecosystems.
- ★ All organisms are composed of cells, the fundamental units of life.
- ★ Cells carry on the many functions needed to sustain life.
- Specialized cells perform specialized functions in multicellular organisms. Groups of specialized cells cooperate to form a tissue, such as a muscle. Different tissues are in turn grouped together to form larger functional units, called organs. Each type of cell, tissue, and organ has a distinct structure and set of functions that serve the organism as a whole.

## Related Ideas in *Benchmarks for Science Literacy* (AAAS 1993)

. . . . . . . . . . . . . . . . . . . . . . . . . . . . . .

### K–2 Basic Functions

- The human body has parts that help it

seek, find, and take in food when it feels hungry: eyes and a nose for detecting food, legs to get to it, arms to carry it away, and a mouth to eat it.

### 3–5 Cells

- Microscopes make it possible to see that living things are mostly made up of cells. Some organisms are made of a collection of similar cells that benefit from cooperating. Some organisms' cells vary greatly in appearance and perform very different roles in the organism.

### 6–8 Cells

- Various organs and tissues function to serve the needs of cells for food, air, and waste removal.
- Cells repeatedly divide to make more cells for growth and repair.
- ★ Within cells, many of the basic functions of organisms—such as extracting energy from food and getting rid of waste—are carried out. The way in which cells function is similar in all living organisms.

### 6–8 Basic Functions

- Organs and organ systems are composed of cells and help to provide all cells with basic needs.
- For the body to use food for energy and building materials, the food must first be digested into molecules that are absorbed and transported to cells.
- To burn food for the release of energy stored in it, oxygen must be supplied to

---

★ Indicates a strong match between the ideas elicited by the probe and a national standard's learning goal.

cells, and carbon dioxide removed. Lungs take in oxygen for the combustion of food and they eliminate the carbon dioxide produced. The urinary system disposes of dissolved waste molecules, the intestinal tract removes solid wastes, and the skin and lungs rid the body of heat energy. The circulatory system moves all these substances to or from cells where they are needed or produced, responding to changing demands.

- Specialized cells and the molecules they produce identify and destroy microbes that get inside the body.

## Related Research

- Preliminary research indicates that it may be easier for students to understand that the cell is the basic unit of structure than that the cell is the basic unit of function. This may be because the former is observable whereas the latter needs to be inferred from experiments (AAAS 1993).
- Research conducted by Dreyfus and Jungwirth (1988) revealed that high school students may have various misconceptions about cells after traditional instruction on cell topics.
- Studies of children's ideas related to the organization of the human body reveal that between the ages of 8 and 10 children begin to understand that the body is made up of organs that work together to maintain life (Driver et al. 1994).
- Many children think that only certain parts of the human body and other living

things are composed of cells (Driver et al. 1992).

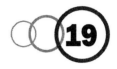

**Topic: Body Systems**
**Go to: www.scilinks.org**
**Code: USIS143**

## Suggestions for Instruction and Assessment

- Before students are asked questions that relate to structure and function, be sure they can distinguish between the two. Have them practice using the word *structure* whenever they refer to any part of an organism or the whole organism. Help them relate the term *function* to the job that is performed and practice using the word in context.
- As middle school students learn about the various body systems, include experiences that specifically show the relationship between a particular body part's structure and its function *at all levels* of complexity. For example, when examining the structure and function of the biceps and triceps muscles in order to understand how the arm moves, provide opportunities to examine the structure and function of muscle tissue and individual muscle cells.
- Decrease emphasis on definitions and memorization of body parts and increase emphasis on structure and function relationships. Continuously tie structure to function and vice versa throughout instruction of the various body systems. Use "Structure and Function" as the overarching theme with the human body as the context. Engage students in activities that constantly revisit this central idea. Always

ask what the function is of a particular system, organ, tissue, or cell. Trace functions of organs and tissues back to the cellular level when possible.

- Integrate the study of the cell into human body system lessons. Often the cell is taught as a separate unit and students fail to make a link between what happens in the human body and in cells.

- Teaching from a systems approach includes examining the parts and functions of all aspects of the system. Using the *Benchmarks for Science Literacy* (1993) section on systems (pp. 262–266) and the *Atlas of Science Literacy* (2001) map on systems (p. 133) to plan instruction may help students better understand parts-and-wholes relationships such as how cells relate to body systems.

- Understand that it is difficult for students to move from the macro view of the processes of life they learn in elementary grades (as well as what they observe in themselves and other organisms) to processes that occur at an invisible, cellular level. If students have learned the basic processes of life and accept a cell as something that is living, then the next logical step is to link those ideas together in middle school to help them understand that cells perform those processes. This idea becomes further developed in high school when students learn the specific details of how cell parts perform the cellular functions.

- Using analogies or metaphors at this level may help. For example, if the human body were represented by a shopping mall, ask students to think of what the body systems, organs, tissues, and cells would represent in terms of both structure and function.

## Related NSTA Science Store Publications and NSTA Journal Articles

American Association for the Advancement of Science (AAAS). 2001. *Atlas of science literacy.* (See "Cells and Organs," pp. 74–75, and "Systems," pp. 132–133.) New York: Oxford University Press.

Driver, R., A. Squires, P. Rushworth, and V. Wood-Robinson. 1994. *Making sense of secondary science: Research into children's ideas.* London and New York: RoutledgeFalmer.

Keeley, P. 2005. *Science curriculum topic study: Bridging the gap between standards and practice.* Thousand Oaks, CA: Corwin Press.

### Related Curriculum Topic Study Guides
(Keeley 2005)
"Cells"
"Human Body Systems"

## References

American Association for the Advancement of Science (AAAS). 1993. *Benchmarks for science literacy.* New York: Oxford University Press.

American Association for the Advancement of Science (AAAS). 2001. *Atlas of science literacy.* New York: Oxford University Press.

Dreyfus, A., and E. Jungwirth. 1988. The cell concept of tenth graders: Curricular expectations and reality. *International Journal of Science Education* 10 (2): 221–229.

Driver, R. et al. 1992. *Life and living processes: Leeds national curriculum support project, Part 2.* Leeds, UK: Leeds City Council and the University of Leeds.

Driver, R., A. Squires, P. Rushworth, and V. Wood-Robinson. 1994. *Making sense of secondary science: Research into children's ideas.* London and New York: RoutledgeFalmer.

Keeley, P. 2005. *Science curriculum topic study: Bridging the gap between standards and practice.* Thousand Oaks, CA: Corwin Press.

National Research Council (NRC). 1996. *National science education standards.* Washington, DC: National Academy Press.

# Functions of Living Things

The functions listed below are performed by living organisms. Which functions are performed by plants, animals, or both? Mark each example with a P, A, or B.

Put a **P** in front of the functions performed *only* by plants.

Put an **A** in front of the functions performed *only* by animals

Put a **B** in front of the functions performed by *both* plant and animals.

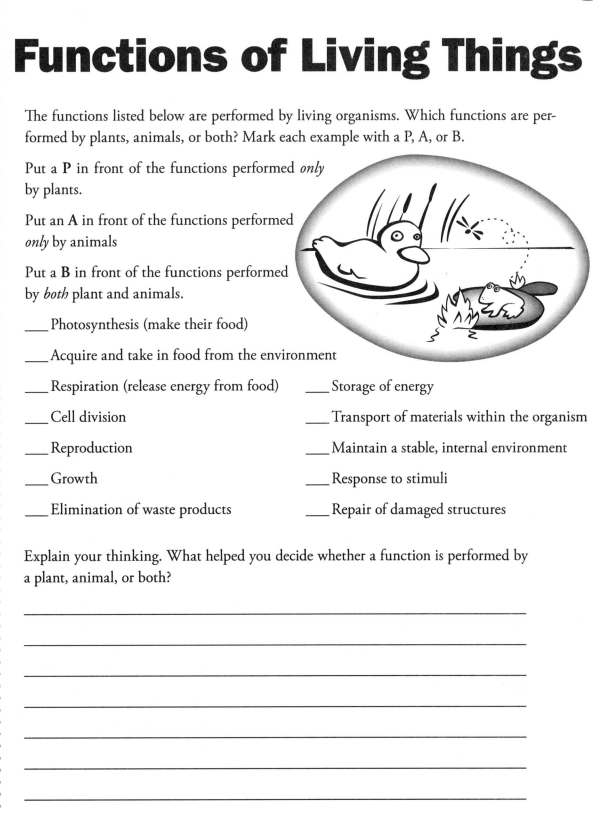

___ Photosynthesis (make their food)

___ Acquire and take in food from the environment

___ Respiration (release energy from food)      ___ Storage of energy

___ Cell division      ___ Transport of materials within the organism

___ Reproduction      ___ Maintain a stable, internal environment

___ Growth      ___ Response to stimuli

___ Elimination of waste products      ___ Repair of damaged structures

Explain your thinking. What helped you decide whether a function is performed by a plant, animal, or both?

_____

_____

_____

_____

_____

_____

_____

_____

# Functions of Living Things

## Teacher Notes

### Purpose

The purpose of this assessment probe is to elicit students' ideas about the functions carried out by plants and animals for maintaining life. The task specifically seeks to find out if students recognize that plants and animals share several common life functions, even though they are seemingly very different organisms.

### Related Concepts

life processes, photosynthesis, respiration

### Explanation

The function performed by plants only is photosynthesis. The function performed by animals only is acquiring and taking in food from the environment. All other functions listed are performed by both plants and animals. Respiration, which is sometimes erroneously referred to as the opposite of photosynthesis, is the process that plants and animals use to release energy from their food. It is carried out in the mitochondria inside their cells. All organisms, including plants, need energy from food in order to live, regardless of whether they make their own or acquire it from the environment. Both plants and animals grow, which is the result of cell division. Even though their methods of reproduction differ, both plants and animals reproduce in order to maintain their species. Waste products, such as gases and water, that are the by-products of chemical reactions within cells are released by both plants and animals. In addition, animals release unused materials from the food they consume.

Topic: Respiration
Go to: *www.scilinks.org*
Code: USIS149

Both plants and animals store energy in the form of carbohydrates or fats resulting from the transformation of food matter for later use. Plants store food in structures such as roots and seeds. Animals store food energy in their body fat. Both plants and animals transform matter in order to repair damaged body structures such as a cut in the skin or a stem. Both plants and animals must transport gases, water, and food molecules throughout the organism. For example, plants use xylem and phloem to transport water and food. Animals have a circulatory system to supply oxygen and transport food molecules. Both plants and animals must maintain a stable internal environment such as a balance between water and salts, and warm-blooded animals must maintain a certain body temperature. Both react to stimuli. An animal's nervous system involves various senses that detect changes and signal the body to respond. Plants have various tropisms that react to gravity and changes in the amount of light and water.

Overall, plants and animals perform similar functions because these are functions needed to maintain cell activities, regardless of whether the cell is a plant or animal cell. The major difference is in activities related to their nutrition. Plants can make their own food but animals must seek it and take it into their bodies. Some students will argue that carnivorous plants, like Venus flytraps, acquire and take in food from their environment. These plants make their own food through the process of photosynthesis using their leaves, just like other plants. The rea-

son they trap insects is to extract the minerals they need for cell processes. These minerals (nutrients) may not be present in the nutrient-poor soil these types of plants grow in, so over time they have adapted to extracting their nutrients from living organisms. These nutrients are analogous to the vitamins we consume. They provide us with essential compounds needed to carry out cell functions but they aren't a source of energy (food). Confusion often arises because we use words like *nutrients* and *food* interchangeably.

## Curricular and Instructional Considerations

### Elementary Students

Students are learning to distinguish between plants and animals based on their needs and basic characteristics. An understanding of cellular processes is a sophisticated topic that isn't addressed until middle school. If this probe is used with upper elementary students, it may be useful in gathering information about ideas that form early on, before students encounter formal instruction in the topics.

### Middle School Students

Students distinguish between plant and animal nutrition, acquisition, and use. They also develop an understanding of basic life processes carried out by a variety of organisms, including plants and animals. This is the time when

**Topic: Photosynthesis**
**Go to: www.scilinks.org**
**Code: USIS150**

students begin to develop ideas about similarities in the needs and functions of different living things. These ideas are grade-level expectations in the national standards. This probe is useful in identifying students' ideas prior to and after instruction about the processes that unite plants and animals as well as the different processes connected to their nutrition.

## High School Students

Students have acquired a more sophisticated understanding of the life processes, particularly the ways they are carried out within cells. This probe is useful in determining students' ideas prior to instruction, particularly whether some students are holding on to the idea that plants and animals perform very different functions and what their reasoning is.

## Administering the Probe

In some examples a descriptive term was included along with the technical term in order to elicit students' understanding that does not rely on vocabulary. You may choose to replace descriptions with technical terms (e.g., *homeostasis*, *mitosis* and *meiosis*, *excretion*), but be aware that students may recognize a process but not the term. This task can also be done as a card sort, allowing the teacher to listen as students discuss their ideas about where to place a function. With elementary students the list can be adapted to include only the basic processes they would recognize at their level.

## Related Ideas in *National Science Education Standards* (NRC 1996)

. . . . . . . . . . . . . . . . . . . . . . . . . . . . .

### K–4 The Characteristics of Organisms

- Each plant or animal has different structures that serve different functions in growth, survival, and reproduction.

### 5–8 Structure and Function in Living Systems

★ Cells carry on the many functions needed to sustain life. They grow and divide, thereby producing more cells. This requires that they take in nutrients, which they use to provide energy for the work that cells do and to make the materials that a cell or an organism needs.

### 5–8 Reproduction and Heredity

★ Reproduction is a characteristic of all living systems.

### 5–8 Regulation and Behavior

★ All organisms must be able to obtain and use resources, grow, reproduce, and maintain stable internal conditions while living in a constantly changing external environment.

### 9–12 The Cell

- Inside the cell is a concentrated mixture of thousands of different molecules that form a variety of specialized structures that carry out such cell functions as energy production, transport of molecules, waste

---

★ Indicates a strong match between the ideas elicited by the probe and a national standard's learning goal.

disposal, synthesis of new molecules, and the storage of genetic material.

## 9–12 Matter, Energy, and Organization in Living Systems

★ Plants capture energy by absorbing light and using it to form strong chemical bonds between the atoms of carbon-containing molecules. These molecules can be used to assemble larger molecules with biological activity. In addition, the energy stored in bonds between atoms can be used as sources of energy for life processes.

• The complexity and organization of organisms accommodates the need for obtaining, transforming, transporting, releasing, and eliminating the matter and energy used to sustain the organism.

## 9–12 The Behavior of Organisms

• Organisms have behavioral responses to internal changes and to external stimuli.

## Related Ideas in *Benchmarks for Science Literacy* (AAAS 1993)

. . . . . . . . . . . . . . . . . . . . . . . . . . . . . .

### K–2 Diversity of Life

• Some animals and plants are alike in the way they look and in the things they do, and others are very different from one another.

### K–2 Cells

• Most living things need water, food, and air.

## 3–5 Cells

• Some living things consist of a single cell. Like familiar organisms, they need food, water, and air; a way to dispose of waste; and an environment they can live in.

## 6–8 Diversity of Life

★ One of the most general distinctions among organisms is between plants, which use sunlight to make their own food, and animals, which consume energy-rich foods.

## 6–8 Cells

• Cells repeatedly divide to make more cells for growth and repair. Various organs and tissues function to serve the needs of cells for food, air, and waste removal.

★ Within cells, many of the basic functions of organisms—such as extracting energy from food and getting rid of waste—are carried out. The way in which cells function is similar in all living organisms.

## 6–8 Flow of Matter and Energy

★ Food provides the fuel and building material for all organisms. Plants use the energy from light to make sugars from carbon dioxide and water. This food can be used immediately or stored for later use. Organisms that eat plants break down the plant structures to produce the materials and energy they need to survive.

## 9–12 Cells

★ Within every cell are specialized parts for the transport of materials, energy transfer,

---

★ Indicates a strong match between the ideas elicited by the probe and a national standard's learning goal.

protein building, waste disposal, information feedback, and even movement.

## Related Research

- Although photosynthesis is recognized as a plant function, many students hold on to a persistent heterotrophic view that plants not only make their own food, but also obtain it from the environment. For example, many students think plants extract food from soil or plant food added to soil (Driver et al. 1994).

- Respiration is regarded as something animals do, not plants. Haslam and Treagust (1987) found that many students, including those at the high school level, often equate respiration with breathing. Interviews with students age nine and older show they use a plant-breathing, animal-breathing model: Animals breathe in oxygen and breathe out carbon dioxide and plants breathe in carbon dioxide and breathe out oxygen. Respiration is often overlooked as an energy releasing process and many students, even college biology students, think photosynthesis is the way plants use and release energy (Driver et al. 1994).

- Students understand that food is necessary for life but have difficulty understanding the connection between food and functions such as growth, repair, storing and releasing energy, and transforming matter. This difficulty is further confounded by alternate views of the purpose for food in plants compared with animals (Driver et al. 1994).

- Some ideas about growth are not based

on cell division, but rather on a basic observational notion of things getting larger (Driver et al. 1994).

## Suggestions for Instruction and Assessment

- Develop ideas about function before introducing the technical terms.

- Beginning in middle school, distinguish between cellular respiration and breathing.

- Be careful in describing photosynthesis and respiration or the carbon dioxide/oxygen cycle as opposite or reciprocal processes. Doing so inadvertently develops the idea that the former occurs in plants with the purpose of providing oxygen to animals and the latter occurs only in animals.

- Use multiple contexts when teaching about life processes. Even though an animal or plant may be used to describe a function, be explicit about other examples (even extending to fungi, protists, and bacteria). In elementary grades, connect ideas to prior instruction. For example, if students studied animals one year and plants another, be sure to connect the animal and plant ideas.

- Use compare and contrast with different types of organisms and explicitly develop the idea of ubiquity—that all organisms perform certain common functions to stay alive and maintain their species, regardless of the obvious differences in external features. This can begin in early elementary grades with basic functions like growth, reproduction, obtaining food from the environment, and responding to the environment.

- In middle school, begin connecting the idea of function to cells—that most functions needed to maintain life occur within cells. By high school, students understand that similar structures in the cells of different organisms perform similar functions.

- Be careful that assessments that are intended to provide information about students' understanding of life processes do not focus exclusively on plant or animal examples.

## Related NSTA Science Store Publications and NSTA Journal Articles

American Association for the Advancement of Science (AAAS). 2001. *Atlas of science literacy.* (See "Flow of Matter in Ecosystems," pp. 76–77.) New York: Oxford University Press.

Driver, R., A. Squires, P. Rushworth, and V. Wood-Robinson. 1994. *Making sense of secondary science: Research into children's ideas.* London and New York: RoutledgeFalmer.

Keeley, P. 2005. *Science curriculum topic study: Bridging the gap between standards and practice.* Thousand Oaks, CA: Corwin Press.

### Related Curriculum Topic Study Guides
(Keeley 2005)
"Characteristics of Living Things"
"Life Processes and Needs of Organisms"
"Photosynthesis and Respiration"
"Regulation and Control"
"Reproduction, Growth, and Development"

## References

American Association for the Advancement of Science (AAAS). 1993. *Benchmarks for science literacy.* New York: Oxford University Press.

Driver, R., A. Squires, P. Rushworth, and V. Wood-Robinson. 1994. *Making sense of secondary science: Research into children's ideas.* London and New York: RoutledgeFalmer.

Haslam, F., and D. Treagust. 1987. Diagnosing secondary students' misconceptions of photosynthesis and respiration in plants using a two-tier multiple choice instrument. *Journal of Biological Education* 21 (3): 203–211.

Keeley, P. 2005. *Science curriculum topic study: Bridging the gap between standards and practice.* Thousand Oaks, CA: Corwin Press.

National Research Council (NRC). 1996. *National science education standards.* Washington, DC: National Academy Press.

# Wet Jeans

Sam washed his favorite pair of jeans. He hung the wet jeans on a clothesline outside. An hour later the jeans were dry.

Circle the answer that best describes what happened to the water that was in the wet jeans *an hour later.*

**A** It soaked into the ground.

**B** It disappeared and no longer exists.

**C** It is in the air in an invisible form.

**D** It moved up to the clouds.

**E** It chemically changed into a new substance.

**F** It went up to the Sun.

**G** It broke down into atoms of hydrogen and oxygen.

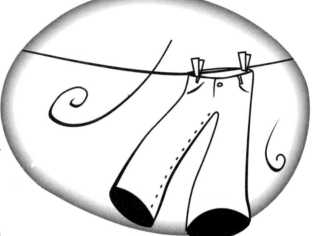

Describe your thinking. Provide an explanation for your answer.

_____

_____

_____

_____

_____

_____

_____

_____

_____

_____

# Wet Jeans

## Teacher Notes

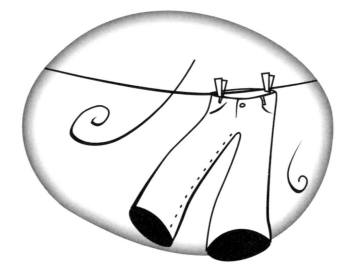

### Purpose

The purpose of this assessment probe is to elicit students' ideas about where water goes right after it evaporates. It is designed to determine if students recognize that water exists in the air around us in the form of water vapor. Since students often use the terminology of the water cycle with little understanding of actual phenomena, this probe intentionally avoids use of technical words such as *evaporation* and *water vapor* in order to examine how students think about evaporation and the water cycle.

### Related Concepts

water cycle, evaporation

### Explanation

The best response is C—it is in the air in an invisible form. This invisible form is called water vapor. Contrary to what is often inadvertently depicted in water cycle diagrams, water does not immediately go up to the clouds or Sun as described in distracters D and F. It rises and exists in the air around us as an invisible gas. Humid weather is an example of water in the air. The wet dew on the grass in the morning or condensation of water on the outside of a cold beverage glass confirms that water exists in the air around us. Eventually some water molecules do rise high in the atmosphere and form clouds. The idea in distracter A that the water from the jeans may have soaked into the ground can be challenged with the observation that water is not dripping off of the wet jeans and landing on the ground. The principle of conservation of matter refutes distracter B.

Topic: Water Cycle
Go to: www.scilinks.org
Code: USIS157

Matter cannot be destroyed. A change in state from a liquid to a gas is a physical change. The substances, liquid water and water vapor, are still chemically the same. They do not change into a new substance or break down into hydrogen and oxygen atoms as described in distracters E and G.

## Curricular and Instructional Considerations

### Elementary Students

Younger students' opportunities to learn focus primarily on phenomena they can observe, such as the notion that water in an open container will eventually disappear. As students progress to upper elementary grades they begin to conduct investigations to explain the observations they made in earlier grades. An important idea to develop before they move on to middle school is the notion that when water disappears it is in the air in the form of invisible water vapor. This is a grade-level expectation in national standards that is often overlooked when teaching the water cycle and emphasizing terminology without understanding. In addition students must have opportunities to learn that air is a substance rather than existing as "nothing." This probe can be used to determine what students' ideas are prior to designing instruction that will help them discover that water goes into the air after it evaporates.

### Middle School Students

The water cycle is of profound importance for middle school students' understanding of Earth systems. However, before the idea of the cyclic nature of water is developed, teachers need to be sure students understand what happens to water after a change in state. Many middle school students use the term *evaporation* without completely understanding where the water goes after it evaporates. Representations of the water cycle in textbooks that show an arrow pointing up to a cloud may perpetuate the idea that evaporated water immediately goes up to the clouds or the Sun. Middle school is the time when students begin to develop a particulate model of what happens to water when it evaporates. This probe is useful in determining whether students have an accurate conception of where water goes after it evaporates from a surface, prior to developing the more sophisticated ideas about cycling of water.

### High School Students

At this level students develop more sophisticated ideas about particulate models and cycling of matter, such as water, through ecosystems. However, do not assume that students have a correct conception of simpler ideas such as evaporation. This probe is useful in determining whether students have progressed beyond their preconceptions about where water goes after it evaporates before more complex ideas are taught in high school Earth science.

### Administering the Probe

If the context of wet laundry on a clothesline is

unfamiliar to students, use a more familiar example such as a puddle drying up after it rains (although this may increase the number of responses that the water soaks into the ground, which points out a strong alternative conception). Or, hang a moist paper towel up in the classroom, which will dry fairly quickly without dripping. This can be combined with students actually observing the phenomenon and then asking the question, Where is the water now? You may wish to ask students to draw a picture to help explain their thinking. The picture helps reveal whether students' thinking is influenced by the diagrams they have seen of the water cycle.

## Related Ideas in *National Science Education Standards* (NRC 1996)

. . . . . . . . . . . . . . . . . . . . . . . . . . . . . .

### K–4 Properties of Objects and Materials

★ Materials can exist in different states: solid, liquid, and gas. Some materials, such as water, can be changed from one state to another by heating or cooling.

### 5–8 Structure of the Earth System

• Water, which covers the majority of the Earth's surface, circulates through the crust, oceans, and atmosphere in what is known as the "water cycle." Water evaporates from the Earth's surface, rises and cools as it moves to higher elevations, condenses as rain or snow, and falls to the surface where it collects in lakes, oceans, soil, and in rocks underground.

## Related Ideas in *Benchmarks for Science Literacy* (AAAS 1993)

. . . . . . . . . . . . . . . . . . . . . . . . . . . . . .

### K–2 The Earth

• Water left in an open container disappears, but water in a closed container does not disappear.

### 3–5 The Earth

★ When liquid water disappears, it turns into a gas (vapor) in the air and can reappear as a liquid when cooled, or as a solid if cooled below the freezing point of water. Clouds and fog are made of tiny droplets of water.

### 6–8 The Earth

• Water evaporates from the surface of the Earth, rises and cools, condenses into rain or snow, and falls again to the surface.

## Related Research

• Research has shown that students seem to go through a series of stages before they fully understand evaporation as a process that converts water to an invisible form. At first they may seem to think that when water evaporates, it simply ceases to exist. In the next stage they may think it changes location but that it changes into some other form we can perceive, such as fog, steam, or droplets. Fifth grade is about the time that students can accept air as the location of evaporating water if they have had special instruction that targets this idea (AAAS 1993).

---

★ Indicates a strong match between the ideas elicited by the probe and a national standard's learning goal.

- Students' scientific concept of evaporation appears to be dependent on three notions: (1) conservation of matter, (2) the idea of atoms or molecules, and (3) the idea that air contains particles we cannot see. Ages 12–14 are the time when students are apt to link these notions (Driver et al. 1994).

- A study by Barr and Travis (1991) found that students' understanding of evaporation in a boiling context may precede their understanding of evaporation of water from surfaces. In the sample in that study, 70% of six- to eight-year-old students understood that there was vapor coming out of water when it boiled. They understood that the water was going somewhere as the amount decreased from the container and that the vapor was made of water. However, the same children thought that when a solid, wet object dried, the water simply disappeared or it went into the object (Driver et al. 1994).

## Suggestions for Instruction and Assessment

- Elementary students should have multiple experiences in observing how water disappears from various surfaces and open containers. Older elementary students should be challenged to think about where the water goes immediately after it disappears and where it may eventually end up.

- Elementary students learn that water in an open container disappears. This is a grade-level expectation in national standards. However, be sure students understand that

the word *disappear* does not mean the water no longer exists but rather that it exists but we can no longer see it. Use an analogy such as a student leaving the room. We can say the student "disappeared" because we can no longer see the student. However, the student still exists somewhere. It is important to be careful how we use words such as *disappear*. Students may develop incorrect notions of conservation of matter in the context of the water cycle if teachers are not careful with the words they use to describe phenomena.

- Elementary students need concrete experiences to understand what happens to water during a change in state before developing the more sophisticated idea of a cycle.

- Teach students what happens to water before introducing terminology like *evaporation*. Many students will use the word *evaporation* without understanding where water actually goes. Students need inquiry-based experiences to discover for themselves that water is in the air around them before using the terminology. The careful wording in *Benchmarks* (AAAS 1993) affirms this notion of developing some ideas before using terminology. Once students have the idea, the term can be introduced with meaning.

- Be aware that many textbook representations may contribute to the idea that evaporated water immediately goes up to the clouds or the Sun. Many representations show upward arrows pointing to the clouds or Sun that may influence students'

thinking about the phenomenon. Explicitly point out the flaw in these representations to students or challenge students to examine representations and point out possible flaws.

- Consider combining an outdoor example with an indoor example. The latter may help students change their thinking that the water went immediately up to the Sun or clouds. For example, a wet paper towel that dries in the classroom during a class period may elicit the question, "Where is the water now?" The confines of the room may help students change their model about where the water goes.

- Challenge older students to come up with an explanation for why wet laundry takes much longer to dry on a humid day. Challenge students to use a particulate model to explain their thinking.

- Some students may have used a humidifier at home or put out pans of water to increase humidity in the air for their houseplants. Use these examples to develop the idea that water molecules are in the air, even though we cannot see them.

- Teaching about evaporation in the water cycle involves several interrelated ideas that should be combined in instruction. These ideas include conservation of matter, phase change, and composition and nature of air. It is particularly important that students accept the idea of air being a substance that is made up of matter we cannot see.

- Many assessment items use water cycle diagrams to determine students' ideas about

the water cycle. Students may answer questions correctly related to the water cycle yet fail to understand the idea that water may exist in the air that surrounds us. Use a variety of items that combine assessment of ideas related to components of the water cycle with assessment of cyclic ideas.

## Related NSTA Science Store Publications and NSTA Journal Articles

American Association for the Advancement of Science (AAAS). 2001. *Atlas of science literacy.* (See "States of Matter," pp. 58–59.) New York: Oxford University Press.

Driver, R., A. Squires, P. Rushworth, and V. Wood-Robinson. 1994. *Making sense of secondary science: Research into children's ideas.* London and New York: RoutledgeFalmer.

Gilbert, S. W., and S. W. Ireton. 2003. *Understanding models in earth and space science.* Arlington, VA: NSTA Press.

Keeley, P. 2005. *Science curriculum topic study: Bridging the gap between standards and practice.* Thousand Oaks, CA: Corwin Press.

Smith, M., and J. Southard. 2002. Water is all around you. *Science Scope* (Oct.): 32–35.

### Related Curriculum Topic Study Guides
(Keeley 2005)
"Water Cycle"
"States of Matter"

## References

American Association for the Advancement of Sci-

ence (AAAS). 1993. *Benchmarks for science literacy.* New York: Oxford University Press.

Barr, V., and A. Travis. 1991. Children's views concerning phase changes. *Journal of Research in Science Teaching* 28 (4): 363–382.

Driver, R., A. Squires, P. Rushworth, and V. Wood-Robinson. 1994. *Making sense of secondary science: Research into children's ideas.* London and New York: RoutledgeFalmer.

Keeley, P. 2005. *Science curriculum topic study: Bridging the gap between standards and practice.* Thousand Oaks, CA: Corwin Press.

National Research Council (NRC). 1996. *National science education standards.* Washington: DC: National Academy Press.

# Beach Sand

Three friends were walking along a beach in New England. They looked closely at the sand and noticed it was made up of tiny particles of rock. They had different ideas about where the sand came from.

Molly: "I think the sand came from distant mountains and landforms."

Fidel: "I think the sand came from rocks on the ocean floor."

Lynn: "I think the sand came from undersea mountains and sea floor formations."

Which friend do you agree with and why? Explain your thinking about how the sand formed *and* ended up on the beach.

_____

_____

_____

_____

_____

_____

_____

# Beach Sand

## Teacher Notes

## Purpose

The purpose of this assessment probe is to elicit students' ideas about weathering, erosion, deposition, and landforms. It is designed to determine if students recognize that sand on a beach may have come from distant mountains and landforms as a result of the weathering of rock, subsequent erosion, and deposition.

## Related Concepts

weathering, erosion, deposition, rock cycle, landforms

## Explanation

Molly's idea is the best response. In this example the beach sand is formed from the wearing away of rock at the Earth's surface. The weathered rock is carried away by wind and water (eroded) where it eventually ended up in the ocean. The small particles of rock were tossed about by the ocean, washing up on the beach as sediment. While it intuitively appears that the sand originated from the ocean, which is partially correct, it actually came from somewhere else before ending up in the ocean. Wind and rain constantly erode mountain summits, hillsides, and other landforms that are made up of rocks. These rocks are composed of many common minerals, such as quartz, feldspar, and mica. The small pieces of rock and minerals, such as quartz, find their way into streams and eventually the mouth of rivers where they are washed out to sea. Currents can carry the sediments many miles away, eventually depositing them along a shoreline. Many of the world's beaches are made up of quartz-rich sand. When you walk along a beach you may be walking on tiny grains from mighty mountains, far away from the shoreline. Although there are exceptions, such as coral beaches, and other complex processes are involved, this probe addresses, at a simple level, how a common type of beach is formed as a result of weathering of landforms.

## Curricular and Instructional Considerations

. . . . . . . . . . . . . . . . . . . . . . . . . . . .

### Elementary Students

Students come to school aware that the Earth is made up of a variety of materials and landforms. Children are encouraged to observe materials in their environment, such as sand, and develop their own explanations of how they came to be. They observe elementary processes of the rock cycle and begin to construct an understanding that rocks, as well as landforms, undergo change. The ideas that rock is eroded by waves, wind, and water; that sand is a small particle of rock; and that rock particles can be carried away and deposited in other areas is a grade-level expectation in the national standards. This probe can be used to find out students' early ideas about weathering and erosion before they put the more complex pieces together in middle school Earth science.

### Middle School Students

Students develop more complex understandings about weathering, erosion, and sedimentation, including the long periods of time it takes for these processes to occur. They use the idea of a rock cycle to explain the continuous process of wearing down and building up. They begin to

use ideas about geologic processes to explain formation of a variety of landforms, including beaches. The idea that the Earth's surface is shaped by the actions of water and wind over long periods of time is a grade-level expectation in the national standards. This probe can be used to assess how students use their ideas about weathering, erosion, and sedimentation to explain processes that result in weathering of mountains and formation of landforms, such as a beach. While students may describe the processes, the notion that the sand may have come from distant mountains may be counterintuitive, and points out the need to design instruction that explicitly targets this phenomenon.

**Topic: Rock Cycle**
**Go to: *www.scilinks.org***
**Code: USIS165**

### High School Students

Students use their understandings of the rock cycle, geologic processes, and the timescales involved to explain complex phenomena that involve changes in the Earth system. They also investigate a variety of other factors that affect beach formation over time and examine different types of beaches. This probe is useful in determining if students have grasped fundamental ideas about weathering, erosion, and deposition in the middle school standards before they encounter more sophisticated concepts related to beach formation.

### Administering the Probe

Be aware that some students may have never visited a coastal area, similar to the context used in this probe, which would affect their

notions of what a beach is and how it was formed. Some students may have visited volcanic beaches or island beaches where shell and coral reef material predominates. Be sure students understand the context the probe is set in. You may change it to a setting that is more familiar to your students, such as a beach in Texas or California, if the context matches the ideas in the probe. You might include additional props, such as photos of the area that show mountains and rivers in the distance or have students examine the particles in sand. This probe may be used with "Mountain Age" (p. 169) to elicit ideas about weathering of rock in a different context.

## Related Ideas in *National Science Education Standards* (NRC 1996)

### K–4 Changes in the Earth and Sky

- The surface of the Earth changes. Some changes are due to slow processes, such as weathering and erosion.

### 5–8 Structure of the Earth System

- ★ Landforms are the result of a combination of constructive and destructive forces. Constructive forces include crustal deformation, volcanic eruption, and deposition of sediment, while destructive forces include weathering and erosion.

- Some changes in the solid Earth can be described as the "rock cycle." Old rocks at the Earth surface weather, forming sediments that are buried, then compacted, heated, and often recrystallized into new rock.

## Related Ideas in *Benchmarks for Science Literacy* (AAAS 1993)

### K–2 Processes That Shape the Earth

- Chunks of rock come in many sizes and shapes, from boulders to grains of sand and even smaller.

### 3–4 Processes That Shape the Earth

- ★ Waves, wind, water, and ice shape and reshape the Earth's land surface by eroding rock and soils in some areas and depositing them in other areas, sometimes in seasonal layers.

### 5–8 Processes That Shape the Earth

- ★ Some changes in the Earth's surface are abrupt (such as earthquakes and volcanic eruptions) while other changes happen very slowly (such as uplift and wearing down of mountains). The Earth's surface is shaped in part by the motion of water and wind over very long times, which acts to level mountain ranges.

### 9–12 Processes That Shape the Earth

- The formation, weathering, sedimentation, and reformation of rocks constitute a continuing "rock cycle" in which the total amount of material stays the same as its form changes.

---

★ Indicates a strong match between the ideas elicited by the probe and a national standard's learning goal.

## Related Research

- Earth (and space) sciences have a unique aspect of scale that may be problematic for students. For example, comprehending the length of time it takes for mountains to erode is difficult for some students (Ault 1994).

- A study by Freyberg (1985) revealed that many students think the Earth today is the same as it has always been and that any changes to the Earth (such as formation of a beach) were sudden and comprehensive. However, it is important to note that students in this study did not have formal instruction in the topics addressed (AAAS 1993).

- Happs (1982) found students tend to use different meanings for rock fragments than scientists who classify the fragments by average size. For example, instead of using particle size to distinguish between boulders, gravel, sand, and clay, students associate the particles with their origin. Sand is defined as coming from a beach or desert rather than being a particle of a certain average size (Driver et al. 1994).

## Suggestions for Instruction and Assessment

- Elementary processes of the rock cycle, such as erosion, transport, and deposition, that lead to later understandings of the processes that form beaches can be observed by elementary students using simple materials they can manipulate. Start with observation before explanation.

- Elementary students can examine sand with magnifiers to observe the particles

and compare the pieces to actual rock samples, particularly ones that contain minerals that are recognizable such as quartz or mica. This helps them understand the origin of sand from rock, and the rock can be later traced back to landforms such as mountains and exposed bedrock.

- Be sure to combine students' observations of and interest in certain phenomena, such as tumbling solid rock, or eroding sand in a stream table, with the role the phenomena play in shaping the surface of the Earth (e.g., beaches, wearing down of mountains, widening of rivers).

- When using stream tables to investigate erosion and deposition phenomena, be sure to trace back the origin of the sand. It is also important to explicitly address the fact that the processes the stream tables are modeling in a very short time actually occur over long periods of time. The sedimentation process is understandable and observable but the span of time involved is difficult for students to grasp, particularly up through middle school.

- Combine an understanding of the use of models with understanding the process of beach formation. This is a good time for students to understand how models are used and the benefits as well as limitations of models in illustrating phenomena.

- Challenge students to explain the statement, "When you sink your toes in the sand on a beach you might be feeling the tiny grains of mighty mountains."

- Provide students with a single grain of

sand from a beach and ask them to trace back the origin of the grain of sand. What journey did it take before ending up on the beach? This can be developed into an engaging performance assessment task.

• Help students distinguish between *weathering* and *erosion*. Some students use these terms interchangeably. Weathering is the wearing away whereas erosion is the carrying away.

• Develop the notion that the type of beach formation described in this context occurs in beaches in many places throughout the world, not just in New England. Be sure students aren't limited by context.

## Related NSTA Science Store Publications and NSTA Journal Articles

American Association for the Advancement of Science (AAAS). 2001. *Atlas of science literacy.* (See "Changes in the Earth's Surface," pp. 50–51.) New York: Oxford University Press.

Driver, R., A. Squires, R. Rushworth, and V. Wood-Robinson. 1994. *Making sense of secondary science: Research into children's ideas.* London and New York: RoutledgeFalmer.

Gilbert, S. W., and S. W. Ireton. 2003. *Understanding models in earth and space science.* Arlington, VA: NSTA Press.

Keeley, P. 2005. *Science curriculum topic study: Bridging the gap between standards and practice.* Thousand Oaks, CA: Corwin Press.

McDuffie, T. 2003. Sand: Up close and amazing. *Science Scope* (Sept.): 31–35.

Sexton, U. 1997. Science learning in the sand. *Science and Children* (Jan.): 28–31, 40–42.

**Related Curriculum Topic Study Guides**
(Keeley 2005)
"Landforms"
"Processes That Change the Surface of the Earth"

## References

American Association for the Advancement of Science (AAAS). 1993. *Benchmarks for science literacy.* New York: Oxford University Press.

Ault, C. R. 1994. Research in problem solving in earth science. In *Handbook of research on science teaching and learning,* ed. D. Gabel. New York: Simon and Schuster.

Driver, R., A. Squires, R. Rushworth, and V. Wood-Robinson. 1994. *Making sense of secondary science: Research into children's ideas.* London and New York: RoutledgeFalmer.

Freyberg, P. 1985. Implications across the curriculum. In *Learning in science,* eds. R. Osborne and P. Freyberg. Auckland, New Zealand: Heinemann.

Happs, J. C. 1982. Rocks and minerals (working paper No. 204). Hamilton, New Zealand: University of Waikato, Science Education Research Unit. (ERIC Document Service No. ED 236 034)

Keeley, P. 2005. *Science curriculum topic study: Bridging the gap between standards and practice.* Thousand Oaks, CA: Corwin Press.

National Research Council (NRC). 1996. *National science education standards.* Washington, DC: National Academy Press.

# Mountain Age

Mountain A                     Mountain B

Mountain A is 4,800 feet tall, looks smooth and rounded, and is located in North America. Mountain B is 19,280 feet tall, looks sharp and jagged, and is located in South America. Both mountains were originally formed by the uplifting of the Earth's crust millions of years ago, are composed of similar material, and are found in similar climate conditions.

Put an X next to the statement that best describes your thinking about the age of the two different mountains based on their shape and height.

_____ Mountain A is probably younger than Mountain B.

_____ Mountain A is probably older than Mountain B.

_____ Mountains A and B are the same age.

Describe your thinking. Provide an explanation for your answer.

_____

_____

_____

_____

_____

# Mountain Age

## Teacher Notes

Mountain A

Mountain B

## Purpose

The purpose of this assessment probe is to elicit students' ideas about processes that affect the shape of mountains. While determining the relative age of mountains involves a variety of complex interacting factors, this probe is designed to determine if students consider weathering factors or if they intuitively believe taller mountains are older.

## Related Concepts

weathering, erosion, landforms

## Explanation

There is no single correct answer to this probe because shape and height alone cannot be used to determine the age of mountains. However, the probe is useful in recognizing the role of weathering and erosion in shaping landforms

such as mountains. Mountains are formed as the result of uplift of the Earth's crust or volcanic activity. While it makes intuitive sense to students that taller mountains are older, mountains cannot be accurately compared for age based on height and shape alone. Several variables are involved in the shape and height of mountains. Weathering and erosion rates may depend on (1) water (e.g., rainfall, freeze-and-thaw cycles, transport), (2) material composition and condition, and (3) other factors such as slope.

Uplifted mountains that are jagged at the top may be relatively young mountains, but they can also be older than smaller rounded mountains. The rock forced upward as the mountain formed over long periods of time has not yet eroded to become smooth. Mountains that are rounded have been subjected to weathering and erosion of rock over long periods of time by water, wind, and ice, causing the mountains to look smooth and rounded. The assumption that one is older than the other cannot be made on appearances alone. However, if the composition and climate conditions are the same, it could be logically inferred that Mountain A may have had more time to be shaped by weathering and erosion.

## Curricular and Instructional Considerations

### Elementary Students

Elementary students' opportunities to learn focus primarily on phenomena they can observe. Students examine changes in Earth materials and build an understanding that surface features of the Earth change due to processes like weathering and erosion caused by wind and water. They begin to develop the notion that some changes are slow and some are rapid. These are grade-level expectations in the national standards. However, the results of processes that happen over long periods of time are difficult for young children to imagine.

### Middle School Students

Middle school students develop more complex understandings about constructive and destructive geologic processes, including the long periods of time it takes for some of these processes to occur. They examine how these forces combine to result in various landforms such as mountains. They begin to use ideas about geo-

logic processes to explain the building up and wearing down of mountains over long spans of geologic time. They recognize the role of water and wind, combined with properties of materials and long spans of time, in shaping mountains. These are grade-level expectations in the national standards. However, students at this age may hold on to preconceived ideas such as mountains grow bigger and taller over time, which explains why many students intuitively select B. This probe is useful in eliciting students' ideas for the purpose of shaping instruction that targets their preconceptions.

### High School Students

Students transition from a descriptive focus on processes that affect the formation and wearing down of mountains to more sophisticated scientific explanations. They combine knowledge about plate tectonics and mountain formation with an understanding of what happens to mountains over long periods of time, including the many variables involved. Students at this level are more apt to grasp the notion of the long periods of time necessary for these processes to occur and the complexity of the factors involved and to understand the evidence that supports these ideas. This probe is useful in determining students' prior understanding of middle school concepts before building on their ideas with more sophisticated concepts.

### Administering the Probe

If students live in an area of the country where familiar mountains can be used as examples (e.g., Appalachian or Rocky Mountains), you

**Topic: Erosion**
**Go to: www.scilinks.org**
**Code: USIS172**

may wish to point them out. Using photos to contrast actual mountains such as Mount Everest and Mount Washington may be more helpful than the small graphics in the probe. This probe may be used with "Beach Sand" (p. 163) to elicit ideas about weathering of rock in a different context.

## Related Ideas in *National Science Education Standards* (NRC 1996)

. . . . . . . . . . . . . . . . . . . . . . . . . . . . . .

### K–4 Changes in the Earth and Sky

• The surface of the Earth changes. Some changes are due to slow processes, such as weathering and erosion.

### 5–8 Structure of the Earth System

★ Landforms are the result of a combination of constructive and destructive forces. Constructive forces include crustal deformation, volcanic eruption, and deposition of sediment, while destructive forces include weathering and erosion.

★ Interactions among the solid Earth, the oceans, the atmosphere, and organisms have resulted in the ongoing evolution of the Earth system. We can observe some changes such as earthquakes and volcanic eruptions on a human timescale, but many processes such as mountain building and plate movements take place over hundreds of millions of years.

## Related Ideas in *Benchmarks for Science Literacy* (AAAS 1993)

. . . . . . . . . . . . . . . . . . . . . . . . . . . . . .

### 3–4 Processes That Shape the Earth

• Waves, wind, water, and ice shape and reshape the Earth's land surface by eroding rock and soils in some areas and depositing them in other areas, sometimes in seasonal layers.

### 5-8 Processes That Shape the Earth

★ Some changes in the Earth's surface are abrupt (such as earthquakes and volcanic eruptions) while other changes happen very slowly (such as uplift and wearing down of mountains). The Earth's surface is shaped in part by the motion of water and wind over very long times, which acts to level mountain ranges.

## Related Research

• Earth (and space) sciences have a unique aspect of scale that may be problematic for students. For example, comprehending the length of time it takes for mountains to erode is difficult for some students (Ault 1994).

• A study by Freyberg (1985) revealed that many students think the Earth today is the same as it has always been and that any changes to the Earth were sudden and comprehensive. However, it is important to note that students in this study did not have formal instruction in the topics addressed (AAAS 1993).

---

★ Indicates a strong match between the ideas elicited by the probe and a national standard's learning goal.

- In summaries of several studies conducted by J. C. Happs in the early 1980s, Driver et al. (1994) indicated that students have a variety of ideas about the composition of mountains and their formation. Children described mountains as "high rocks" or "clumps of dirt or soil." Some students believed all mountains came from volcanoes or molten rock and some believed they were formed from "rock pushed up." Happs's studies revealed that most children in the study were unable to use a theory of mountain building that involved plate tectonics (Driver et al. 1994).

- Stavy and Tirosh (1995) identified intuitive rules students use to reason various problems. The rule "more A, more B" is a common rule students use in their reasoning. In the context of this probe, students may apply this rule and think that because a mountain is taller, then it must be older.

## Suggestions for Instruction and Assessment

- Elementary students can begin by firsthand observations of processes of weathering and erosion by using rock tumblers, water, and sandboxes. Once they grasp the processes of weathering, erosion, and deposition, they can begin to connect these processes to the features of landforms and how they change.

- Elementary and middle school students may confuse growth of organisms with growth of mountains. They may believe mountains grow over time in much the same way that organisms grow and become taller, and fail to recognize the role of weathering and erosion. Comparing and contrasting these two processes may help older students understand why size cannot be an accurate indicator of mountain age.

- Because most students do not have direct experience with the processes that shape the Earth or their long-term nature, some explanations should wait until late in grades 5–8 (NRC 1996).

- Students should have opportunities to see a variety of landforms in photographs and videos and describe how they came to be. Yet, be aware that some pictures may lead to faulty interpretations. For example, students may cite evidence based on observations in pictures that glaciers chip mountains away so the more ragged one is older because glaciers occurred a long time ago.

- Be explicit about the span of geologic time that is necessary for these processes to occur. Yet, understand how difficult it is for elementary and middle school students to imagine these time spans.

- Use models to help students visualize the results of processes that happen over long periods of time.

- Help students link the ideas that different types of materials weather differently and that weather and climate in different regions of the world affect geologic processes. These foundational ideas will help them see why it is difficult to visually determine relative age of mountains based on their size and shape.

- Because an individual mountain is often part of a system of mountains, be sure to include comparisons among mountains within different mountain ranges.

- High school instruction may include the historical episodes that led to the modern understanding of the age of the Earth and that features such as mountains are formed over long periods of time and are still in the process of change. Examining the types of evidence that led to this modern notion will help students accept a modern theory of the geologic processes that change mountains over time.

- Be aware that some popular creationist beliefs may impede students' understanding of how mountains came to be. Some creationist views propose that mountains were formed by a single, instantaneous creation.

- "Because direct experimentation is usually not possible for many concepts associated with earth science, it is important to maintain the spirit of inquiry by focusing the teaching on questions that can be answered by using observational data, the knowledge base of science, and processes of reasoning" (NRC 1996, pp. 188–189).

- Help students distinguish between *weathering* and *erosion*. Some students use these terms interchangeably. Weathering is the wearing away whereas erosion is the carrying away.

## Related NSTA Science Store Publications and NSTA Journal Articles

American Association for the Advancement of Science (AAAS). 2001. *Atlas of science literacy.* (See "Changes in the Earth's Surface," pp. 50–51.) New York: Oxford University Press.

Driver, R., A. Squires, P. Rushworth, and V. Wood-Robinson. 1994. *Making sense of secondary science: Research into children's ideas.* London and New York: RoutledgeFalmer.

Gilbert, S. W., and S. W. Ireton. 2003. *Understanding models in earth and space science.* Arlington, VA: NSTA Press.

Keeley, P. 2005. *Science curriculum topic study: Bridging the gap between standards and practice.* Thousand Oaks, CA: Corwin Press.

Monnes, C. 2004. The strongest mountain. *Science and Children* (Oct.): 35–37.

Stavy, R., and D. Tirosh. 1995. *How students (mis-) understand science and mathematics: Intuitive rules.* New York: Teachers College Press.

### Related Curriculum Topic Study Guides

(Keeley 2005)

"Landforms"

"Processes That Change the Surface of the Earth"

"Weathering and Erosion"

"Models"

## References

American Association for the Advancement of Science (AAAS). 1993. *Benchmarks for science literacy.* New York: Oxford University Press.

Ault, C. R. 1994. Research in problem solving in earth science. In *Handbook of research on science teaching and learning,* ed. D. Gabel. New York: Simon and Schuster.

Driver, R., A. Squires, P. Rushworth, and V. Wood-Robinson. 1994. *Making sense of secondary science: Research into children's ideas.* London and New York: RoutledgeFalmer.

Freyberg, P. 1985. Implications across the curriculum. In *Learning in science,* eds. R. Osborne and P. Freyberg. Auckland, New Zealand: Heinemann.

Keeley, P. 2005. *Science curriculum topic study: Bridging the gap between standards and practice.* Thousand Oaks, CA: Corwin Press.

National Research Council (NRC). 1996. *National science education standards.* Washington, DC: National Academy Press.

Stavy, R., and D. Tirosh. 1995. *How students (mis-) understand science and mathematics: Intuitive rules.* New York: Teachers College Press.

# Gazing at the Moon

Enrico and Leah live in opposite hemispheres. Enrico lives in Santiago, Chile, which is in the Southern Hemisphere. Leah lives in Boston, Massachusetts, which is in the Northern Hemisphere. They both gazed at the Moon on the same evening. Enrico noticed there was a full Moon when he looked up at the sky from his location (the Southern Hemisphere). What do you predict Leah saw when she looked up in the sky from her location (the Northern Hemisphere)?

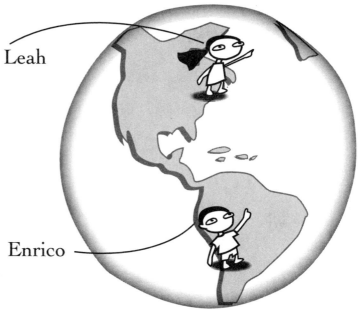

**A** New Moon (no part of the Moon is visible)

**B** Crescent Moon (a quarter of the face of the Moon is visible)

**C** Half Moon (half of the face of the Moon is visible)

**D** Gibbous Moon (three-quarters of the face of the Moon is visible)

**E** Full Moon (the entire face of the Moon is visible)

Provide an explanation for your answer. How did you decide what the Moon would look like in the opposite hemisphere?

_____

_____

_____

_____

_____

# Gazing at the Moon

## Teacher Notes

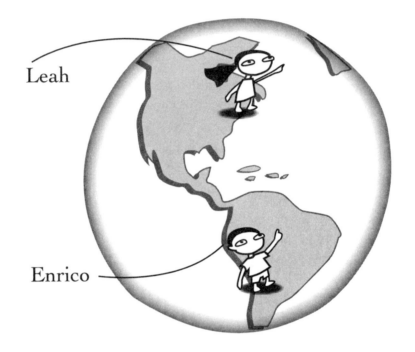

Leah

Enrico

## Purpose

The purpose of this assessment probe is to elicit students' ideas about the Earth, Moon, and Sun system. It is designed to find out if students think Moon phases change with the geographic location of observation. The probe may determine whether students use a rule of "opposites" in their reasoning about Moon phases seen in opposite hemispheres on the same evening.

## Related Concept

phases of the moon

## Explanation

The best response is E—a full Moon. The phase of the Moon seen anywhere on Earth is the same since the positional relationship of the Earth to the Sun and the Moon does not change although your location on Earth differs. The change in your location is not significant enough to change the view of the Moon to a different phase. One logical way to reason this problem without the need to use scientific ideas is to consider a calendar. Many calendars show the phase of the Moon at different days of the year. If the phases of the Moon changed with location, imagine the implications—multiple versions of calendars would have to be designed specifically for different geographic locations!

## Curricular and Instructional Considerations

### Elementary Students

Phases of the Moon are addressed in most elementary curricula. Young children are naturally curious about the Moon. However, it is important to recognize that elementary students' experiences with Moon phases should be observational, not explanatory. At this level an understanding of Moon-related phenomena involves observing, drawing, and recording the phases of the Moon at regular intervals and noting that there is a repeating pattern but not explaining what causes these changes. This is a grade-level expectation in the national standards. Although the ideas in this probe exceed what elementary students are expected to know and depend on their experience with geographic concepts, it may be useful in determining ideas that develop early on.

### Middle School Students

Students at this age begin to develop more sophisticated ideas about the Earth, Moon, and Sun system and the geometry involved. However, the explanation for Moon phases is still difficult to grasp. Furthermore, students are developing ideas about the cause of seasons, and their geographic knowledge helps them understand that seasons in the Southern Hemisphere are the opposite of the Northern Hemisphere. Ideas about phases of the Moon and seasons progress from an elementary emphasis on observation to explanation in middle school. Both the cause of seasons and the phases of the Moon are grade-level expectations in the national standards. This probe is useful in determining whether students apply the "opposites" rule of the seasons in different hemispheres to their reasoning about Moon phases.

### High School Students

By high school, students are expected to know what causes the phases of the Moon. Even though they may be able to do this, this probe may reveal that they have an incomplete picture of the positional relationships involved in the Earth, Moon, and Sun system.

**Topic: Moon Phases**
**Go to: www.scilinks.org**
**Code: USIS179**

### Administering the Probe

You may choose to provide a labeled graphic showing the Moon phase for each of the distracters. You may wish to point out the different locations on a three-dimensional globe to students, in addition to the map in the graphic. The locations can be changed to further probe students' ideas about geography in relation to the phases of the Moon. For example, you may wish to probe further to see if students think there is a difference between the Eastern and Western Hemispheres or even the north/south or east/west of the United States.

## Related Ideas in *National Science Education Standards* (NRC 1996)

### K–4 Changes in the Earth and Sky

- Objects in the sky have patterns of movement. The observable shape of the Moon changes from day to day in a cycle that lasts about a month.

### 5–8 Earth in the Solar System

- ★ Most objects in the solar system are in regular and predictable motion. Those motions explain such phenomena as the day, the year, phases of the Moon, and eclipses.

## Related Ideas in *Benchmarks for Science Literacy* (AAAS 1993)

### K–2 The Universe

- The Moon looks a little different every day, but looks the same again about every four weeks.

### 6–8 The Earth

- ★ The Moon's orbit around the Earth once in about 28 days changes what part of the Moon is lighted by the Sun and how much of that part can be seen from the Earth—the phases of the Moon.

## Related Research

- Explanations of the phases of the Moon as well as seasons are very challenging to students as well as adults. Students may not be able to understand explanations of these phenomena until they can reasonably grasp ideas about the Earth, Moon, and Sun system, including relative size, motion, and distance (AAAS 1993).
- Our search of the research did not show any studies that equate the opposites model of the seasons in different hemispheres to reasoning about the phase of the Moon seen in different hemispheres. This probe would make an interesting research study.

## Suggestions for Instruction and Assessment

- Elementary students should have opportunities to observe, draw, and record the phases of the Moon in order to develop an understanding of the repeating pattern and predictability of the phenomenon. This is also a time when students can look at calendars to see that these phases are predictable and noted on calendars. This might be a time to point out how these same calendars are used worldwide and have students come up with the logical idea that everyone must see the same Moon phase regardless of where they live without explaining the positional relationships too early on.
- Models are important for helping students understand the positional relationship that allows us to see the phases of the Moon. When using models with middle school students to demonstrate how we see different phases of the Moon, help them see that the same phase is observed from different locations on the Earth.

---

★ Indicates a strong match between the ideas elicited by the probe and a national standard's learning goal.

- If students use the opposites rule that they use with seasons in their explanation, help them see why this rule applies to the seasons because of the tilt of the Earth and not to the phases of the Moon.

## Related NSTA Science Store Publications and NSTA Journal Articles

American Association for the Advancement of Science (AAAS). 2001. *Atlas of science literacy.* (See "Solar System," pp. 44–45.) New York: Oxford University Press.

Driver, R., A. Squires, P. Rushworth, and V. Wood-Robinson. 1994. *Making sense of secondary science: Research into children's ideas.* London and New York: RoutledgeFalmer.

Gilbert, S. W., and S. W. Ireton. 2003. *Understanding models in earth and space science.* Arlington, VA: NSTA Press.

Hermann, R., and B. Lewis. 2003. Moon misconceptions: Bringing pedagogical research of lunar phases into the classroom. *The Science Teacher* (Nov.): 51–55

Keeley, P. 2005. *Science curriculum topic study: Bridging the gap between standards and practice.* Thousand Oaks, CA: Corwin Press.

Lindgren, J. 2003. Why we have seasons and other misconceptions. *Science Scope* (Jan.): 50–51.

Rider, S. 2002. Perceptions about moon phases. *Science Scope* (Nov./Dec.): 48–51.

Smith, S. 2001. *Project earth science: Astronomy.* Arlington, VA: NSTA Press.

Smith, W. 2003. Meeting the moon from a global perspective. *Science Scope* (May): 24–28.

Taylor, I. 1996. Lunar phases: Students construct fundamental knowledge of moon phases. *The Science Teacher* (Nov.): 39–41.

Volkmann, M., and S. Abell. 2003. Seamless assessment. *Science and Children* (May): 41–45.

### Related Curriculum Topic Study Guide
(Keeley 2005)
"Earth, Moon, and Sun System"

## References

American Association for the Advancement of Science (AAAS). 1993. *Benchmarks for science literacy.* New York: Oxford University Press.

Keeley, P. 2005. *Science curriculum topic study: Bridging the gap between standards and practice.* Thousand Oaks, CA: Corwin Press.

National Research Council (NRC). 1996. *National science education standards.* Washington, DC: National Academy Press.

# Going Through a Phase

Mrs. Timmons asked her class to share their ideas about what causes the different phases of the Moon. This is what some of her students said:

Mona: The Moon lights up in different parts at different times of the month.

Jared: The phases of the Moon change according to the season of the year.

Sofia: Parts of the Moon reflect light depending on the position of the Earth in relation to the Sun and Moon.

Drew: The Earth casts a shadow that causes a monthly pattern in how much of the Moon we can see from Earth.

Trey: Different planets cast a shadow on the Moon as they revolve around the Sun.

Oofra: The shadow of the Sun blocks part of the Moon each night causing a pattern of different Moon phases.

Natasha: The clouds cover the parts of the Moon that we can't see.

Raj: The Moon grows a little bit bigger each day until it is full and then it gets smaller again. It repeats this cycle every month.

Which student do you agree with and why? Explain your thinking.

_____

_____

_____

_____

_____

# Going Through a Phase

## Teacher Notes

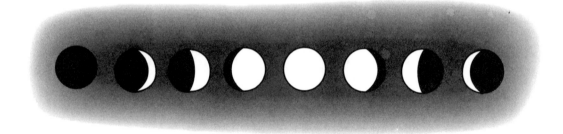

## Purpose

The purpose of this assessment probe is to elicit students' ideas as to what accounts for the phases of the Moon. It is designed to find out if students recognize the role of light reflection and the positional relationship between the Earth, Moon, and Sun in understanding why we see different phases of the Moon.

## Related Concept

phases of the Moon

## Explanation

Sofia has the best answer. The Moon does not emit light. The moonlight we see from Earth is actually light coming from the Sun that is reflected off the Moon's surface. Approximately half of the Moon is usually illuminated by the Sun; the portion (face) of the Moon that is illuminated depends on the positions of the Sun and Moon. The portion of the lit face of the Moon that can be seen from Earth depends

on relative positions of the Earth, Moon, and Sun. As the Moon moves in its orbit around the Earth, different portions of it appear to be lit up, as we look at it from our relative position on Earth. This is why we see the different phases of the Moon. There is no shadow involved except for the unlit side of the Moon that is in its own shadow. The important idea is that the Moon itself doesn't change, nor does the amount of the Moon that is lit by the Sun change. The only thing that changes is the position of the Moon relative to the Earth and the Sun, which gives us our view. This change in relative position results in the different phases of the Moon. These phases repeat in a predictable pattern as the Moon revolves around the Earth.

## Curricular and Instructional Considerations

### Elementary Students

Phases of the Moon are addressed in most el-

ementary curricula. Young children are naturally curious about the moon. However, it is important to recognize that elementary students' experiences with Moon phases should be observational, not explanatory. At this level an understanding of Moon-related phenomena involves observing, drawing, and recording the phases of the Moon at regular intervals and noting that there is a repeating pattern but not explaining what causes these changes. This is a grade-level expectation in the national standards. Although the ideas in this probe exceed what elementary students are expected to know, it can be used to determine intuitive ideas students have that begin to form well before they encounter formal explanations for Moon phases in middle school.

## Middle School Students

Students at this age begin to develop ideas about the Earth, Moon, and Sun system. However, the reason why we see different Moon phases is still a difficult idea to grasp (even for adults), even though it is a grade-level expectation in the national standards. This probe is useful in determining the various conceptual models students use to explain the phases of the Moon for the purpose of designing instruction that challenges these ideas.

## High School Students

By high school, students are expected to know what causes the phases of the Moon. However, even after formal instruction in middle school, students may revert to their preconceived notions. This probe is useful in determining

if students have a correct conception of the phases of the Moon and whether further instruction is needed before proceeding to more sophisticated astronomy concepts.

## Administering the Probe

You may choose to begin this probe by having students observe, draw, and describe the phases of the Moon they see over a given period of time. Their experience can be used to justify which of the distracters are the correct explanations for their observations.

## Related Ideas in *National Science Education Standards* (NRC 1996)

. . . . . . . . . . . . . . . . . . . . . . . . . . . . . .

### K–4 Changes in the Earth and Sky

* Objects in the sky have patterns of movement. The observable shape of the Moon changes from day to day in a cycle that lasts about a month.

### 5–8 Earth in the Solar System

★ Most objects in the solar system are in regular and predictable motion. Those motions explain such phenomena as the day, the year, phases of the Moon, and eclipses.

## Related Ideas in *Benchmarks for Science Literacy* (AAAS 1993)

. . . . . . . . . . . . . . . . . . . . . . . . . . . . . .

### K–2 The Universe

* The Moon looks a little different every day, but looks the same again about every four weeks.

---

★ Indicates a strong match between the ideas elicited by the probe and a national standard's learning goal.

### 6–8 The Earth

★ The Moon's orbit around the Earth once in about 28 days changes what part of the Moon is lighted by the Sun and how much of that part can be seen from the Earth—the phases of the Moon.

## Related Research

- Explanations of the phases of the Moon are very challenging to students as well as adults. Students may not be able to understand explanations of these phenomena until they can reasonably grasp ideas about the Earth, Moon, and Sun system, including relative size, motion, and distance (AAAS 1993).

- Baxter (1989) investigated students' ideas about phases of the Moon and identified five predominant ideas, including the correct one (which is that a portion of the Moon reflects light depending on our position in relation to the Sun and Moon). All four of the incorrect ideas involved a shadow: (1) clouds cover part of the Moon, (2) planets cast a shadow on the Moon, (3) the shadow of the Sun falls on the Moon, and (4) the shadow of the Earth falls on the Moon.

- In a study by Philip Sadler (1987), 37% of the students sampled thought the phases of the Moon were caused by the Earth's shadow.

## Suggestions for Instruction and Assessment

- Elementary students' experiences should be focused on opportunities to observe, draw, and record the phases of the Moon in order to develop an understanding of the repeating pattern and predictability of the phenomenon. It is too early to ask students to explain what causes the phases of the Moon.

- Combine experiences learning about light reflection and light sources with understanding how we see parts of the Moon at night. Students need to understand that light is reflected by the Sun and that we see part of the reflection. It also dispels the notion some students have that the Moon lights up from the inside.

- This is an example of a phenomenon that is best explained and understood using physical models. However, for students, merely observing a model the teacher presents is less effective than constructing, using, and making sense of one's own model.

- Comparing the lunar eclipse phenomenon using a model to explain the phases of the Moon may help students see why the shadow notion works for the eclipse but not phases of the Moon. Comparing and contrasting the two different phenomena with middle school students may help students better understand why the shadow model does not support the phases of the Moon.

## Related NSTA Science Store Publications and NSTA Journal Articles

American Association for the Advancement of Science (AAAS). 2001. *Atlas of science literacy* (See

---

★ Indicates a strong match between the ideas elicited by the probe and a national standard's learning goal.

"Solar System," pp. 44–45.) New York: Oxford University Press.

Driver, R., A. Squires, P. Rushworth, and V. Wood-Robinson. 1994. *Making sense of secondary science: Research into children's ideas.* London and New York: RoutledgeFalmer.

Gilbert, S. W., and S. W. Ireton. 2003. *Understanding models in earth and space science.* Arlington, VA: NSTA Press.

Hermann, R., and B. Lewis. 2003. Moon misconceptions: Bringing pedagogical research of lunar phases into the classroom. *The Science Teacher* (Nov.): 51–55.

Keeley, P. 2005. *Science curriculum topic study: Bridging the gap between standards and practice.* Thousand Oaks, CA: Corwin Press.

Lindgren, J. 2003. Why we have seasons and other misconceptions. *Science Scope* (Jan.): 24–28.

Rider, S. 2002. Perceptions about moon phases. *Science Scope* (Nov./Dec.): 48–51.

Smith, S. 2001. *Project earth science: Astronomy.* Arlington, VA: NSTA Press.

Taylor, I. 1996. Lunar phases: Students construct fundamental knowledge of moon phases. *The Science Teacher* (Nov.): 39–41.

Volkmann, M., and S. Abell. 2003. Seamless assessment. *Science and Children* (May): 41–45.

**Related Curriculum Topic Study Guide**
(Keeley 2005)
"Earth, Moon, and Sun System"

## References

American Association for the Advancement of Science (AAAS). 1993. *Benchmarks for science literacy.* New York: Oxford University Press.

Baxter, J. 1989. Children's understanding of familiar astronomical events. *International Journal of Science Education* 11(Special Issue): 502–513.

Keeley, P. 2005. *Science curriculum topic study: Bridging the gap between standards and practice.* Thousand Oaks, CA: Corwin Press.

National Research Council (NRC). 1996. *National science education standards.* Washington, DC: National Academy Press.

Sadler, P. 1987. Misconceptions in astronomy. Paper presented at the Second International Seminar: Misconceptions and Educational Strategies in Science and Mathematics, July 26-29, Cornell University.

# Index